GLOBAL DEMOCRACY AND THE WORLD SOCIAL FORUMS

GLOBAL DEMOCRACY AND THE WORLD SOCIAL FORUMS

Jackie Smith
Marina Karides
Marc Becker
Dorval Brunelle
Christopher Chase-Dunn
Donatella della Porta
Rosalba Icaza Garza
Jeffrey S. Juris
Lorenzo Mosca
Ellen Reese
Peter (Jay) Smith
Rolando Vázquez

Paradigm Publishers
Boulder • London

Copyright © 2008 Paradigm Publishers

Published in the United States by Paradigm Publishers, 3360 Mitchell Lane, Suite E, Boulder, CO 80301 USA.

Paradigm Publishers is the trade name of Birkenkamp & Company, LLC, Dean Birkenkamp, President and Publisher.

Library of Congress Cataloging-in-Publication Data
Global democracy and the World Social Forums / Jackie Smith . . . [et al.].
    p.   cm. — (International studies intensives)
  Includes bibliographical references and index.
  ISBN 978-1-59451-420-3 (hc : alk. paper) — ISBN 978-1-59451-421-0 (pbk : alk. paper)   1. World Social Forum.   2. Social movements—International cooperation.   3. Anti-globalization movement—International cooperation.
4. International economic relations.   5. Democracy.   6. Globalization—Social aspects.   I. Smith, Jackie, 1968–
  HN18.3.G543 2007
  306.309'0511—dc22

                                        2007014913

Printed and bound in the United States of America on acid-free paper that meets the standards of the American National Standard for Permanence of Paper for Printed Library Materials.

11   10   09   08   07   1   2   3   4   5

To those daring and creative enough
to imagine a different world and
courageous enough to help make it a reality

CONTENTS

ILLUSTRATIONS

Maps

Tables

Preface and Acknowledgments

We know what you're against, but what are you *for*?" It was a question that inspired the creation of the World Social Forum process, which may prove to be the most important political development of the twenty-first century. The World Social Forum (WSF) process is composed of an annual global meeting, complemented by hundreds of regional, national, and local social forums. It all began in Porto Alegre, Brazil, in 2001, when more than 15,000 activists—more than three times the number expected—gathered, united by the slogan "Another World Is Possible."

Since then it has met in other cities of the global south, including Mumbai, Caracas, Karachi, Bamako, and Nairobi. This choice of meeting places reflects an explicit attempt on the part of WSF organizers to make voices and perspectives of the global south more central to global policy discussions. Readers will note that our book displays rotated images of the globe to emphasize how our worldviews are shaped by arbitrary conventions that privilege northern perspectives.

The global forum now draws upward of 150,000 participants, and the proliferation of smaller regional, national, and local forums continues. Organizers see the WSF process as creating an "open space" for citizens to explore the negative impacts of global restructuring on their local and national experiences while expanding transnational dialogues and social movement networking to address shared problems. The WSF is a space and process for those wanting another kind of global integration that emphasizes human needs over economic growth, environmental protection over corporate profits, and social inclusion over a competitive economic race to the bottom. In a global system where opportunities for citizen participation are rare, the WSF serves as a laboratory for global democracy. Activists are testing new forms of political participation and representation that might eventually help democratize global institutions.

This book is designed to help people understand the significance of the World Social Forum process for the future of democracy, and we write primarily for an audience largely unfamiliar with the WSF and the social forum process. The coauthors of this volume build on extensive research on social movements, globalization, and the World Social Forums. Collectively, we have attended all of the World Social Forums and dozens of regional and local forums as researchers, organizers, and participants. The scholars writing here are committed to the WSF process as offering the world a promising new form of politics to meet the ever growing demands for justice, peace, and equality in a global economy. Although we work in our professional associations and in our communities to carry out the work advanced by the WSF process, we remain critical in our study and analysis of the WSF. Due to this and the engagement of our scholarship, the volume offers a rich understanding of the WSF that encapsulates not only its initial impetus but also the tensions that drive the process.

We have not only learned about the WSF process through our engagement with it, but we have also tried to use the lessons of the WSF to advance new ways of developing knowledge and communicating research findings. This book is a truly collaborative project, and *twelve* of us actually *did* write this book together. Just as the forum is an iterative gathering of social change advocates who are seeking new ways to communicate, work together, and engage in global politics, this book allowed us to have an ongoing dialogue through our writing and editing of a common text. We found new, cooperative ways of writing that helped us appreciate things we otherwise would not have seen. We had to trust each other to come through under very strict deadlines, and we built a sense of community as a result of our collaboration, despite the fact that not all of us have ever met in person and most of our work happened at a distance. Although not intentional, this is strikingly representative of the WSF process.

The book chapters build on each other to provide readers a precise but vivid picture of the WSF. The first chapter considers the rise of one of the most distinctive forms of political organizing of our time and presents an understanding of the global context in which the WSF emerged. Chapters 2, 3, 4, and 5, the bulk of the volume, are each devoted to examining issues that have received particular scrutiny by those who study and participate in the WSF. These include concerns with openness of participation, the scale of activity, access and fairness in decision-making processes, and the range of solutions and alternatives that participants propose, learn from, and continue to build. The last chapter offers a brief consideration of the future prospects of the first U.S. Social Forum, which will be held shortly before the publication of this book.

Each of us has benefited from various sources of support for our research on the World Social Forum process, and we acknowledge this support. Most immediately, for their support for a workshop on the WSF process, which was held at the University of Notre Dame in 2006, we are grateful to the following offices: The Joan B. Kroc Institute for International Peace Studies, the Institute for Scholarship in the Liberal Arts in the College of Arts and Letters, the Center for the Study of Social Movements and Social Change, the Office of Research, and the Department of Sociology at the University of Notre Dame. The Notre Dame workshop helped bring together a growing network of scholars working to expand scholarly attention to the WSF process and to strengthen interdisciplinary and cross-national collaboration in this area. We expect this book to represent just the first of many new cooperative projects that will advance both the understanding and the practice of global democracy.

Support for travel and other research needs of the book's coauthors was provided by the World Society Foundation; the Office of the Vice President of Research and the Dean of Arts and Sciences at Stony Brook University; Dorothy F. Schmidt, College of Arts and Letters of the Florida Atlantic University; the Observatory of the Americas at the University of Quebec in Montreal; the Institute for Research on World Systems at the University of California–Riverside; the Italian Ministry for Research and the University; the European Commission; the Wenner-Gren Foundation for Anthropological Research, Inc.; the Social Science Research Council; the Athabasca University Academic Research Fund; and the Sociology Departments at Gothenburg University and Warwick University. Massimiliano Andretta and Herbert Reiter contributed to the Democracy in Europe and the Mobilization of Society (DEMOS) project's research on the European Social Forums. And the following people helped with the University of California–Riverside survey research project cited in this book: Rebecca Alvarez, Toi Carter, Erika Gutierrez, Mark Herkenrath, Matt Kaneshiro, Linda Kim, Richard Niemeyer, Christine Petit, Darragh White, and undergraduate interns enrolled in Sociology 197 at the University of California–Riverside.

Chapter One
GLOBALIZATION AND THE EMERGENCE OF
THE WORLD SOCIAL FORUMS

In the 1970s and 1980s, protests against the lending policies of the International Monetary Fund (IMF) emerged in the global south. By the late 1990s, tens of thousands of protesters were gathering wherever the world's political and economic elite met, raising criticisms of global economic policies and calling for more just and equitable economic policies. As the numbers of protesters grew, so did the violence with which governments responded. Governments spent millions and arrested hundreds of nonviolent protesters to ensure their meetings could take place. Italian police killed Carlo Giuliani, a twenty-three-year-old protester, at the meeting of the Group of 8 (G8) in Genoa in 2001, dramatizing for activists in the global north the brutal repression against activists that is common in the global south. The size of police mobilizations against these overwhelmingly nonviolent protests was unprecedented in Western democracies, and it signaled the declining legitimacy of the system of economic globalization promoted by the world's most powerful governments. After years of such protests against the world's most powerful economic institutions—the World Bank, the International Monetary

Fund, the World Trade Organization (WTO), and the G8—a team of Latin American and French activists launched the first World Social Forum (WSF) in January 2001.

Over just a few short years, the WSF has become the largest political gathering in modern history and a major focal point of global efforts to promote an alternative vision of global integration. Mobilizing around the slogan "Another World Is Possible," the WSF began as both a protest against the annual World Economic Forum (WEF) in Davos, Switzerland, and as an effort to develop a shared vision of alternatives to the predominant, market-based model of globalization. Many see the WSF as a crucial process for the development of a global civil society that can help democratize the global political and economic order, and some would argue that it is the most important political development of our time. This book aims to introduce readers to the WSF process—by which we mean the networked, repeated, interconnected, and multilevel gatherings of diverse groups of people around the aim of bringing about a more just and humane world—and the possibilities and challenges this process holds. In this chapter we describe the political and economic conditions that gave rise to the global justice movement and the WSF.

The first WSF was held in Porto Alegre, Brazil, in late January 2001. The timing of the WSF was strategically chosen to coincide with the WEF, an annual meeting of global political and economic elites typically held in Davos, Switzerland. The WEF is a private interest group that has worked since its founding in 1971 to promote dialogue among business leaders and governments and to shape the global economy. Over the years an ever-more-impressive list of political leaders have participated in this private event, for which corporate members pay upward of $15,000 for the opportunity to schmooze with the global power elite. Civil society has been largely shut out of the process of planning an increasingly powerful global economy.

The WEF is widely criticized for providing a space where the future of the world is decided while excluding the democratic participation of most of the globe's population. French and Latin American activist groups and political organizations were among the first to protest the WEF in 1999. This eventually blossomed into the idea of a WSF that received sponsorship in Brazil from the Worker's Party, a political party that won government elections in the city of Porto Alegre, supported the principles of global economic justice, and was willing to work with social change activists to coordinate the first WSF.

This first meeting in Porto Alegre, Brazil, drew more than twice the 4,000 people organizers anticipated, and the global meeting now regularly attracts more than 150,000 registered participants. Its first attempt to move outside of Porto Alegre was in 2004 when the WSF met in Mumbai, India. After a return to Porto Alegre in 2005, it moved to Africa (Nairobi) in 2007 in an effort to expand opportunities for different activists to participate. Inspired by the call for open discussions of and organizing around visions of "another world," activists launched regional and local counterparts to the WSF around the world. This expanded opportunities for citizens to become part of the WSF process and helped sustain and energize local organizing efforts.

The WSF has become an important, but certainly not the only, focal point for the global justice movement. It is a setting where activists can meet their counterparts from other parts of the world, expand their understandings of globalization and of the interdependencies among the world's peoples, and plan joint campaigns to promote their common aims. It allows people to actively debate proposals for organizing global policy while nurturing values of tolerance, equality, and participation. And it has generated some common ideas about other visions for a better world. Unlike the WEF, the activities of the WSF are crucial to cultivating a foundation for a more democratic global economic and political order.

The WSF not only fosters networking among activists from different places, but it also plays a critical role in supporting what might be called a transnational counterpublic (Olesen 2005; cf. Fraser 1992). Democracy requires public spaces for the articulation of different interests and visions of desirable futures. If we are to have a more democratic global system, we need to enable more citizens to become active participants in global policy discussions. Without a global public sphere, there can be no plural discussion of global issues. Even the most democratic governments lack public input and accountability for actions that influence the living conditions of people in other parts of the world.

Just as the WSF serves as a foundation for a more democratic global polity, it also provides routine contact among the countless individuals and organizations working to address common grievances against global economic and political structures. This contact is essential for helping activists share analyses and coordinate strategies, but it is also indispensable as a means of reaffirming a common commitment to and vision of "another world," especially when day-to-day struggles often dampen such hope. Isolated groups lack information and creative input needed to innovate and adapt their strategies. In the face of repression, exclusion, and ignorance, this transnational solidarity helps energize those who challenge the structures of global capitalism. While many activists will never have the chance to attend the global WSF meeting, they see themselves as part of the process and know they are not alone in their struggles. Aided by the Internet and an increasingly dense web of transnational citizens' networks, the WSF and its regional and local counterparts dramatize the unity among diverse local struggles and encourage coordination among activists working at local, national, and transnational levels.

The Global Scene: Politics and Economy in the Neoliberal Era

Globally and nationally, the logic of the relationship between governments and corporations changed somewhere between the late 1970s and the early 1980s (McMichael 2003; Brunelle 2007). The global justice movement and the WSF challenge the economic and political restructuring initiated during this period, which is seen as increasing social inequalities, environmental degradation, and political injustices worldwide. In this section, we review how global economic restructuring taking hold in the mid-1980s undermined democracy and transformed the globe.

Changes in the World's Economic Principles

For fifty years up until the mid-1980s the ideas of John Maynard Keynes dominated economic policymaking. The principles of Keynes, or Keynesianism, included two very important features that informed economic policies in the United States and the world in the aftermath of the Great Depression. First, government involvement in economic development was encouraged as vital to successful capitalist industrialization (Portes 1997; McMichael 2003). Government duties included providing a buffer against cyclical economic downturns and planning and developing various economic sectors (Kiely 1998; Portes 1997; McMichael 2003). Second, government was also needed to reduce the inevitable inequalities produced by capitalist development. Such redistribution and assistance would not—according to Keynesian principles—interfere with economic growth, but rather it would help foster it.

The Keynesian era and the organization of the global political economy on these principles ended in the mid-1980s and were replaced with what is widely referred to as the Washington Consensus (Williamson 1997), or neoliberalism. Former U.S. president Ronald Reagan and former U.K. prime minister Margaret Thatcher are two leading politicians responsible for ushering in the neoliberal era. Neoliberals argue that prioritizing the interest of capital is the only assurance for national economic success. Governments were required to drastically reduce their involvement with the economy, and good governance was measured by the extent to which a state could promote development through market forces. Government attempts at poverty alleviation and the reduction of social inequality were viewed as detrimental to economic growth. Neoliberal proponents view all regulations on corporate activity, such as those that protect the environment from toxic dumping or workers from unsafe and unhealthy working conditions, as a hindrance to economic growth.

Proponents of economic globalization like to argue that if governments enact policies to encourage international trade and economic growth (profits) for corporations, the benefits will automatically "trickle down" to all sectors of society. One of the claims made by those advocating a free-market model for global economic governance is that, if progress is to be achieved, *there is no alternative* (TINA) to the global expansion of capitalism. Margaret Thatcher made precisely this claim. Neoliberals have shaped the policies of global institutions like the World Bank, the International Monetary Fund, and the World Trade Organization to promote this particular vision of global economic integration. Because those adopting this model of economic development occupied positions of power within the world's richest and most powerful countries, they were able to effectively impose the neoliberal model of globalization from above. They did this through the terms of international aid and loans and through unequal trading arrangements (McMichael 2003; Peet 2003; Robinson 2004; Babb 2003).

Critics of economic globalization argue that markets alone are not able to achieve many important social goals, such as ensuring a humane standard of living for all people, protecting the natural environment, and limiting inequality. Markets sometimes aid economic growth, and they have succeeded in generating vast amounts of wealth and technological innovation, but they also have contributed to rising global inequalities. Moreover, many experts argue that the recent decades of rapid globalization have not generated economic benefits for most of the world's poor. They point to World Bank and United Nations statistics to demonstrate that, for instance, the poorest 100 countries are actually worse off economically than they were before the 1980s, and that the costs of global economic restructuring have disproportionately affected the world's poorest people (see, e.g., UNDP 2005).

Political Participation on a Global Scale

Given these failures of market-oriented approaches to governing the world economy, participants in the WSF criticize the "democratic deficit" in global institutions. They argue that we need a model of global integration that allows a wider range of people—not just financial experts—to be involved in shaping decisions about how our economic and social lives are organized. Yet along with the economic principles of neoliberalism guiding the current world order is the elite strategy of *depoliticization*, or the deliberate effort to exclude civil society from political participation in global governance.

Depoliticization is driven by the belief that democracy muddles leadership and economic efficiency. This crisis of democracy is reflected in the proliferation of public protests and other forms of citizen political participation, which are seen by the neoliberals as resulting from excessive citizen participation in democracy. In other words, states and governments have been overburdened by democratic demands that increase their involvement in social and economic programs. Through the depoliticization of society, citizens and their organizations, either for profit or nonprofit, are forced through measures such as the privatization of public spaces and political repression to withdraw from a shrinking public sphere. Instead, they are encouraged to operate on their own through market forces. States and governments are not only deemed incapable of tackling issues such as homelessness, housing shortages, or environmental pollution, they are also rendered powerless. Therefore, under neoliberalism, the governance of democracies is not the sole responsibility of elected and accountable governments but, rather, of markets.

How have we come to a world stage where the problems we face are not attributed to faulty economic reasoning and corporate profiteering but to the influence of "nonexpert" citizens on economic and social policy decisions? The crisis of democracy was a diagnosis developed by political and economic elites in the 1970s, a time when the WEF was first launched. Two reports had a profound impact on how governments came to redefine their relations with their citizens and social organizations in the ensuing years. The first was a report made to the Trilateral Commission in 1975, and the second was a 1995 Commission on Global Governance report.

The Trilateral Commission

David Rockefeller, president of the Chase Manhattan Bank, founded the Trilateral Commission in 1973 (Sklar 1980). This initiative was prompted by three sets of events. The first and foremost event was the deterioration of relations among the three economic poles of the capitalist economy (e.g., North America—basically the United States and Canada at the time, the European Community, and Japan) after former U.S. president Nixon removed the U.S. dollar from the gold standard, changing one of the major foundations of the global economy as it was structured since the Bretton Woods Agreement of 1944.

The second event was the growing politicization of Third World nations and the process of decolonization that shattered the control of colonial empires over many regions of the globe. In particular, the Bandung Conference, a meeting in 1955 of newly independent nations that had not officially aligned themselves with either the capitalist or socialist nations, and the founding of the Organization for Solidarity with the Peoples of Africa, Asia, and Latin America (OSPAAAL) in 1966 represented to U.S. economic leaders a potential threat to the country's influence around the globe. The third event that triggered the creation of the Trilateral Commission was the growing student unrest throughout the world in the late 1960s, which was fueled in part by the social revolutions in the Third World and by the growing social opposition to the war in Vietnam.

Soon after its creation, the Trilateral Commission conducted a study to assess what they saw as the ills that were plaguing democracy. The report, *The Crisis of Democracy: Report on the Governability of Democracies to the Trilateral Commission*, provided a framework accepted by many politicians and academics to define and explain the crisis of democracy (Crozier et al. 1975). The report spells out a theory of cycles according to which increasing participation on the part of citizens in political affairs leads to social polarization. In turn, this polarization fosters distrust toward the political process, which leads to a weakening of its efficacy and efficiency, and ultimately, to lower political participation. Consequently, governments should encourage political passivity so that prevailing excessive citizen democratic participation can be reduced. Instead reliance on expertise, experience, and seniority was emphasized as the best model for effective governance.

The Commission on Global Governance

The context leading to the creation of the Commission on Global Governance in 1995 is quite different from the one that gave birth to the Trilateral Commission. However, some of the underlying issues are similar and can help us understand the movement toward depoliticization. Two important precursors were the end of the Cold War and the mission to chart a new course for the United Nations for its fiftieth anniversary.

The growing participation of civil society organizations in UN-sponsored conferences reflected the need for some form of global governance in an increasingly interlinked global economy. For instance, the first Earth Summit held in Stockholm in 1972, which a large number of nongovernmental organizations (NGOs) attended, gained more international prominence than had previous conferences.[1] Running parallel to the official conference was an NGO Forum, which included a daily newspaper providing immediate and often critical coverage of negotiations inside. The summit otherwise would have been much less open to public scrutiny. The Stockholm pattern was repeated, and expanded, at subsequent UN conferences on issues such as population, food, human rights, development, and women (Rice and Ritchie 1995).

Although the first Earth Summit set a precedent for international decisionmaking and global participation, it was the second Earth Summit in 1992 that revealed the difficulties besetting world governance and eventually led to the Commission on Global Governance. The commission report, *Our Global Neighborhood*, acknowledged that national governments had become less and less able to deal with a growing array of global problems. It argued that the international system should be renewed for three basic reasons: to weave a tighter fabric of international norms, to expand the rule of law worldwide, and to enable citizens to exert their democratic influence on global processes (Carlsson and Ramphal 1995). To reach these goals, the commission proposed a set of "radical" recommendations, most notably the reform and expansion of the UN Security Council, the replacement of ECOSOC by an Economic Security Council (ESC), and an annual meeting of a Forum of Civil Society that would allow the people and their organizations, as part of "an international civil society," to play a larger role in addressing global concerns.

The commission report recognized that global governance operates through a complex set of venues at the world level, including the International Monetary Fund, the World Bank, the World Trade Organization, and major partners such as the then Group of 7 (G7), the Organisation for Economic Co-operation and Development (OECD), as well as regional organizations such as the European Union (EU), North American Free Trade Agreement (NAFTA), and Mercosur (the Southern Common Market). The proposed Economic Security Council was to provide a focal point for global economic and social policy, mirroring the intergovernmental structure of the UN Security Council. In one of the most profound statements of the dilemmas with respect to global governance, the report stated:

> At a global level, what model of decision-making should an emerging system of economic governance adopt? It will have to draw on lessons from regional and national levels and from business organizations where inflexible, centralized command-and-control structures have been shown to be unsustainable. Multilayered decision-making systems are emerging that depend on consultation, consensus, and flexible "rules of the games." Intergovernmental organizations, however, still face

basic questions as to who should set the rules and according to what principles. (Commission on Global Governance 1995:146–147)

Significantly, the report also stated that global governance cannot rest on governments or public sector activity alone, but should rely on transnational corporations—which "account for a substantial and growing slice of economic activity" (Commission on Global Governance 1995:153). Whereas it recognized a need for civil society and NGOs to be active in global governance, the report supported the increased role of market forces and the expansion of neoliberal agents of globalization such as the WTO. In effect, it endorsed the notion that business and private enterprise should take a dominant role in global governance, while NGOs and civil society should play a subordinate role assisting governments and business in (market-oriented) development at the local level.

Like the report presented by the Trilateral Commission twenty years prior, the report of the Commission of Global Governance also fails to provide a meaningful role for civil society in global governance. In both reports, society and citizens remain a depoliticized entity. However, our analysis highlights a fundamental contradiction in the globalization program envisioned by the authors of these reports. Although both seek to remove civil society from playing a substantive role in the development of global policy, the Commission on Global Governance recognized that civil society needed to have some role if the institutions of governance were to be seen as legitimate. Without popular legitimacy, the stability of this new international order would be compromised. This tension between the desire to exclude most of the population from policymaking while also strengthening the possibilities for global governance created opportunities for challenges by those denied a voice in shaping the direction of globalization (Markoff 1999).

The WSF: A New Principle of Global Politics

If we consider the increasing privatization, commercialization, and depoliticization of social life and the underlying rational mechanism of efficiency, profit, and accumulation, it appears as if the wheels of history were set in the mid–1980s on an inexorable path toward the dominance of corporations and the eradication of social equality, justice, and political freedom. Given this panorama it would have been difficult to predict the emergence of the WSF as a political body running in a radically different direction. How could we have thought the WSF was possible? Yet contrary to Thatcher's claim that there is no alternative, the WSF arose as a global force, powered by transnational social movements that would have to be reckoned with by governments and corporations. The WSF is an arena for the practice of a democratic form of globalization and a common public space where previously excluded voices can speak and act together to challenge the TINA claim.

The WSF is not simply (or even mainly) a reaction against neoliberal globalization. Instead, it grows from the work of many people throughout history working to advance a just and equitable global order (see Smith 2008). In this sense, it constitutes a new body politic, a common public space where previously excluded voices can speak and act in plurality. With the help of the ideas of noted political theorist Hannah Arendt, we propose to see the WSF not as the logical consequence of global capitalism but rather as the foundation for a new form of politics that breaks with the historical sequence of events that led to the dominance of neoliberal globalization. Arendt viewed the political as a sphere that is not ruled by processes and where the unexpected can happen:

> It is not in the least superstitious, it is even a counsel of realism, to look for the unforeseeable and unpredictable, to be

prepared for and to expect "miracles" in the political realm.
And the more heavily the scales are weighted in favor of disaster, the more miraculous will the deed done in freedom
appear; for it is disaster, not salvation, which always happens
automatically and therefore always must appear to be irre-
sistible. (1993:170)

Precursors to the WSF

If our understanding of the WSF is to be set apart from the
processes of neoliberal globalization, we need to see more con-
cretely the unexpected events that sit at the beginning of this
break in our political history. The WSF is a culmination of political actions for social justice, peace, human rights, labor rights,
and ecological preservation that resist neoliberal globalization
and its attempts to depoliticize the world's citizens. We identify
four key factors that interacted to help set the WSF in motion.
These factors include:

- Third World protests against international institutions;
- Transnational networks and global mobilizations that
  challenged the logic of depoliticization (such as those in
  Seattle in 1999 and Chiapas in 1994);
- Civil society dissatisfaction with the UN system;
- The rise of a transnational feminist and women's move-
  ment.

More than any other global actions or transnational networking, the Zapatista uprising in Chiapas, beginning January
1, 1994, and the anti-WTO protests in Seattle in November
1999 were perhaps the most direct precursors to the WSF. After
discussing the factors listed above, we showcase these two

events to highlight their roles in helping to bring about the WSF process.

Protests in the Global South

The origins of the WSF lie in the countries that have been most deeply impacted by globalization—the countries of the global south. In the 1970s and 1980s, those countries found themselves increasingly squeezed by growing international debts and decreasing prices for the goods they export. They had borrowed money from the World Bank and International Monetary Fund both to cover large-scale industrial development projects as well as to meet the rising costs of fuel during the 1970s successive oil crises. Now these loans were coming due, and they found themselves unable to service their debts while also continuing to develop their national economies and meet the needs of their citizens. Furthermore, the World Bank and IMF began attaching strict conditions to the loans they made, forcing Third World governments to cut government spending and raise interest rates in order to obtain international financing (McMichael 2003). They reasoned that these policies—though painful in the short term—would allow long-term economic growth and, more importantly, ensure that debtor countries could pay back their loans. Essentially, governments had to force their citizens to bear the brunt of the costs of the debt. In many poor countries, this led to what have been called "IMF riots," where citizens protested against the policies of global financial institutions as well as the actions of their own governments (Walton and Seddon 1994).

The IMF riots demonstrated that people in the Third World saw international institutions as a major cause of their economic hardships. Moreover, they saw that their own governments were part of the problem, as their governments were limited in their ability to pursue policies at odds with those favored by the World Bank and IMF. The people also saw that their governments held little sway in those institutions.

Transnational Networks and Global Mobilizations

Meanwhile, in the global north, or the rich Western countries, citizens were organizing around a growing number of environmental problems. Environmentalists and unionists joined forces with each other, and across nations, to contest proposed international free trade agreements, such as the North American Free Trade Agreement (NAFTA) and the Multilateral Agreement on Investment (Ayres 1998; Smith and Smythe 2001). Meanwhile, workers and their allies organized transnational campaigns against the practices of transnational corporations (see, e.g., Sikkink 1986). Northern citizens also became more interested in how the policies of their governments were affecting people elsewhere in the world. Some of this interest grew from the peace and solidarity movements of the 1970s and 1980s (Rucht 2000). The interventionist policies of Western governments encouraged transnational solidarity campaigns between northern activists and their counterparts in the Third World (Gerhards and Rucht 1992; Smith 2008).

At the same time, the United Nations was sponsoring a number of global conferences on issues such as women's rights, environmental protection, and peace that provided opportunities for citizen activists from around the world to meet, exchange stories about their work, and compare analyses of the global and local problems they faced. Aided by advances in technology and reduced costs of transnational communication and travel, these efforts generated more long-term and sustained transnational cooperation than was possible in earlier decades. Beginning in the 1970s there was a tremendous growth in the numbers of formally organized groups working across national borders to promote some kind of social or political change. Thus, between the early 1970s and the late 1990s, the number of transnationally organized social change groups rose from less than 200 to nearly 1,000 (Smith 2004a). Many more transnational citizens' groups were formed around other goals, such as encouraging recreational activities and supporting religious or professional identities, among others. These groups were not only building their own memberships, but they were also forging relationships with other nongovernmental actors and with international agencies, including the United Nations. In the process, they nurtured transnational identities and a broader world culture (Boli and Thomas 1999).

NGO Dissatisfaction with UN Conferences

A third factor that fueled the idea of an alternative venue was the growing dissatisfaction among NGO participants with the mediocre results, if not setbacks, coming out of the conferences convened by the UN—especially the 1992 Conference on Environment and Development (UNCED) in Rio de Janeiro, Brazil; the 1995 Fourth World Conference on Women in Beijing; and the 1995 World Summit on Social Development in Copenhagen. For a number of NGOs that participated in these UN conferences, dissatisfaction changed into disillusionment at the five-year review (dubbed "Rio/Beijing/Copenhagen plus five") conferences aimed at assessing governments' follow-through on the commitments they made at these world conferences. Activists at the review meetings called these the "Rio [or Beijing or Copenhagen] minus five" conferences, highlighting governments' failures to fulfill their conference promises.

Besides their disappointment with the inability of UN conferences to affect the practices of governments, civil society groups that worked hard to influence the texts of the conference agreements felt that much of their efforts in the UN were futile.

The real obstacle, they realized, was not the absence of multilateral agreements, but rather the structure of the UN system and the refusal of major countries to address key global issues. Moreover, they saw that many environmental and human rights agreements were being superseded by the WTO, which was formed in 1994 and which privileged international trade law over other international agreements. Agreements made in the UN were thus made irrelevant by the new global trade order, in which increasingly powerful transnational corporations held sway (Smith 2008).

The Global Women's Movement and Feminist Participation

Women's social movement organizations throughout the world have been very effective in establishing networks to promote international responses to gender injustices and violence against women (Moghadam 2005). While women's organizations continue to participate in UN-led conferences, many are also very active in the WSF. The first of the Feminist Dialogues was held in 2003 in Mumbai, India, as a follow-up to the Women's Strategy Meeting held at the 2002 WSF in Porto Alegre, Brazil, in which feminists from around the world came together to discuss their dissatisfaction with men dominating the WSF. In 2005 and 2007 the Feminist Dialogues preceded the WSF event to provide a space to consider feminist concerns, which many organizations feel are sidelined at the WSF, and to collectively influence the forum (Macdonald 2005). Nevertheless, one of the main contributions of feminist political organizations has been their promotion of the participatory processes that refuse to prioritize one issue over another.

While focusing on gender, feminist activists (especially those from the global south) emphasize the intersection of inequalities such as race, gender, nation, class, and sexuality. In addition, feminist activism challenges hierarchical organizational structures that establish formal leadership that tend to silence the voices of the majority. The history of transnational feminist organizing provided important models for fostering decentralized, respectful dialogue and cooperation that helped inform other social movements seeking to bridge national and other differences (see, e.g., Rupp 1997; Alvarez et al. 2004; Polletta 2002; Gibson-Graham 2006). In fact, the model of the "encuentro," a meeting that is organized around a collectivity of interests without hierarchy, on which the Zapatistas and later the WSF process built, emerged from transnational feminist organizing in Latin America (Sternbach et al. 1992; Smith 2008).

Zapatismo and the Battle of Seattle

Many accounts of the 1994 Zapatistas' uprising in Chiapas, Mexico, and the so-called Battle of Seattle during the WTO ministerial meetings of December 1999 speak of their implications for global democracy and for citizens' mobilizations around the world (Burbach 1994; Harvey 1998; Bello 2000; Gill 2000; Halliday 2000; Kaldor 2000; Seoane and Taddei 2002; Scholte 2000). These two key events helped break the continuity of the processes of neoliberal globalization and, therefore, helped open the possibility for the WSF to emerge as an alternative political body (see Escobar 2004a). The events of Chiapas and Seattle reflect not simply resistance to globalized capitalism, but rather they were catalysts to a new political dynamic within the global landscape.

Zapatismo

In 1994 indigenous people in Mexico took up arms to protest their governments' acceptance of the North American Free Trade Agreement. The Zapatistas quickly emerged as one of the first globally networked groups to resist economic globalization. Their struggle inspired many activists in all parts of the world to more actively resist the growing global trade regime. For many, the emergence of a global citizens' movement is credited to the appearance of the Ejercito Zapatista de Liberación Nacional (EZLN, Zapatista National Liberation Army) on the world scene, January 1, 1994, the same day that NAFTA came into force (Amin et al. 2002; Benasayag and Sztulwark 2002). According to Samir Amin and others, the EZLN ushered in an era of "new radicality" fundamentally different from that which prevailed before then.

Worldwide supporters of the EZLN helped popularize some of the writings of the Zapatista leader, Subcomandante Marcos, which were becoming widely known among activists during the 1990s. When the 1999 Seattle and subsequent protests generated complaints from movement critics that "we know what you're against, but what are you *for*?" Marcos's words proved fruitful in inspiring activists to focus on the quest for alternatives. He argued that one of the main problems of economic globalization is that it does not allow other forms of economic and social organization to coexist. Its need to continually expand and conquer makes it incompatible with the desire for diversity in either nature or society. Marcos argued that we can have "one world with room for many worlds" if we can rein in the movement toward economic globalization. A tolerance for diverse forms of economic organization, a respect for local autonomy and participation in economic decisions, and a celebration of the possibilities for innovation and adaptation fostered by diversity were values that Marcos encouraged (Olesen 2005). The widespread attention to his work demonstrates the transnational resonance of his ideas (Khasnabish 2005).

Following the 1994 EZLN uprising, the Zapatistas used the Internet strategically to call on others to join their struggle for a new sort of world (Cleaver 1995; Ronfeldt et al. 1998). Many around the world responded to their call, and they traveled to Chiapas to participate in international meetings, or "encuentros," on how to confront economic globalization. Many more organized in their local communities in support of Zapatista goals: "against neoliberalism and for humanity" (Schultz 1998). Marcos's analysis of the problems of economic globalization and the possibilities for popular liberation inspired the "political imaginations" of many people facing common experiences in the global neoliberal order (Khasnabish 2005).

The Zapatista uprising and subsequent mobilization are without doubt a cornerstone of the global justice movement. They established and disseminated a pattern of transnational mobilization that continues to inspire and inform activists throughout the world. Moreover, the writings of Marcos and the approach to organizing he promoted provided a focal point that helped bring activists together around a shared understanding of their values and organizing capacities. The networks Zapatismo inspired—including an important grassroots formation called Peoples Global Action—provided an infrastructure of people, organizations, and ideas required for the WSF's emergence. These groups helped catalyze global resistance to the G8 and WTO during the late 1990s, including the June 1999 Global Day of Action Against Capitalism and the November 1999 protests in Seattle (Juris 2008; Notes from Nowhere 2003; Starr 2005).

The Battle of Seattle

As we have seen, the preconditions for the emergence of global justice movements included increasing capacity for globally coordinated action, a growing recognition of the limitations of the UN, the diffusion of feminist organizing principles, and resistance in the global south to international institutions. While these factors percolated in various nations at different rates in numerous social justice organizations, by 1999 the stage was set for the entrance of a new form of political participation.

Unexpectedly for many, the global justice movement seemed to explode on the scene in Seattle in 1999. Tens of thousands of college students, labor union members, educators, public health workers, unemployed workers, environmental activists, feminists, immigrants, and other concerned citizens came to protest the ministerial meetings of the World Trade Organization. The vast majority of activists engaged in peaceful protest, and some sought to nonviolently disrupt the meeting by occupying the streets surrounding the conference hall where WTO delegates were to meet. But police were unprepared for the volume of protesters, and they responded with brutality, triggering what was called "the Battle of Seattle." Although subsequent inquiries showed that the police were at fault by instigating violence against protesters and bystanders, the mainstream media portrayed the protesters as violent and unreasonable (Smith 2002).

A key feature of the organization behind the Seattle protest was the lack of formalized leadership. Rather than a single organization or political body representing the protesters as a single entity, smaller units referred to as affinity groups came together around shared values and identities, uniting with others to forge a common front against the meetings of the WTO. While some affinity groups blocked traffic and engaged in other acts of civil disobedience, trade unionists and other activists marched along preordained march routes and gave passionate speeches denouncing the WTO's policies before a stadium full of supporters. The actions held that day in Seattle were not directed by a single person, group, or organizing unit. Rather they happened organically from the context of protest in which they were situated and from each organization's own traditions of protest.

Global mobilizations like the one in Seattle also present opportunities for learning about the struggles of other groups and understanding the relationship among the organizations attending. For instance, many church members who participated in the Seattle protests learned about the damaging effects of global economic policies through their interactions with other church members around the world. They marched to demand greater equity and justice for all members of their faith (and presumably other faiths as well), regardless of where they were from. Students and teachers that found their schools increasingly impoverished by cuts in public budgets see a connection between their experiences and the changes in the global economy. Unions and professional associations have also been motivated by both threats to their members' interests as well as their solidarity with their counterparts around the world.

Given this rapid growth of transnational networking, by the time of the Seattle WTO meeting many participants had already learned a great deal from each other and had cultivated skills for organizing protests at the local, national, and increasingly the transnational levels. Moreover, subsequent global mobilizations in cities such as Prague, Quebec City, Genoa, Barcelona, and Washington, D.C., continued to provide critical spaces for learning, coalition building, and action. At the same time, many activists felt global protests alone were insufficient. Rather than simply denouncing what they were *against*, it was also important to articulate a clear vision of what they were fighting *for*. In January 2001, the first ever WSF was organized precisely to provide a space for developing concrete alternatives to corporate globalization. Indeed, the WSF process is an important place for popular education about the injustices occurring all over the world as a result of the policies of economic globalization. At the same time, the process creates opportunities for groups to learn about and articulate economic and political alternatives and plan future mobilizations.

Conclusion

Protesters in Seattle and elsewhere and participants in the social forums have challenged people to ask whether the world's major economic institutions are producing the kind of world in which they want to live. The answer, activists argue, is that we cannot govern by markets. Rather, we need political institutions that can help balance competing social interests and goals. By separating trade and other economic policy decisions from other policy areas (such as human rights, public safety, or environmental protection), governments have undermined their own legitimacy and introduced untenable contradictions into international law. Social forum participants argue that the goal of reducing restrictions on international trade must not be allowed to trump other social values and goals.

Governments gain their legitimacy from popular elections and recognition by their populations as their representatives. But with globalization, governments are delegating more policy decisions to international institutions such as the WTO or the European Union. While global interdependence requires some policy coordination to ensure peace and common security, the way governments have managed international policy has created a "democratic deficit" in global institutions. Many of those protesting economic globalization argue for greater government accountability and responsiveness in both domestic and international policy arenas. As they have pursued their particular aims— such as environmental protection, human rights, and equitable development—civil society groups have found themselves uniting behind demands for a more democratic global polity. The protests against economic globalization are really wider battles about whether people and democratic institutions or technical experts and markets should govern the global system.

Understanding the WSF process as a fundamentally new form of politics challenges the visions of history that emphasize chronological chains of processes where all that happens is the logical consequence of its context and its immediate past. Although growing out of a long tradition of struggle, the process of rebellion made visible in Chiapas and Seattle has begun to fracture the historical process of neoliberal domination. The continuity of corporate globalization is now in question. By challenging the relentless progression of privatization, trade liberalization, consumption, and individuation, the rebellion has created another temporality within which the WSF is clearly situated.

The following chapters explore in detail the WSF process. We consider how the process has developed over time, focusing on the creative tensions that have both challenged organizers and helped propel the process forward.

Chapter Two
WHAT ARE THE WORLD SOCIAL FORUMS?

A s the previous chapter indicates, the World Social Forum
(WSF) emerged as a challenge to the broad global changes
that limited space for democratic participation as economic
globalization expanded and deepened. A global wave of protest
against neoliberalism emerged during the 1980s and 1990s as
people pressed for a greater role in defining the course of globalization. The WSF was put forward as an "open space" for
exchanging ideas, resources, and information; building networks
and alliances; and promoting concrete alternatives to neoliberal
globalization. Both *open space* and *networks* are organizational
concepts used by the global justice movement to ensure more
equitable participation than occurs, for instance, in traditional
political parties and unions.

The WSF process emphasizes "horizontality," to increase
opportunities for grassroots participation among members
rather than promote "vertical" integration where decisions are
made at the top and reverberate down. However, organizations
and networks participating in the WSF process can themselves
be either horizontal or vertical in their organizational structures.
The "horizontals" favor decentralized, loosely knit movement

networks and organizations with flat, open, nonhierarchical, and more directly democratic decisionmaking processes. They are self-conscious about prefiguring the type of society they want to create (Juris 2005b). However, they often lack mechanisms to ensure that those actually participating are accountable to, or represent the concerns of, constituents. The verticals, on the other hand, accept the need for hierarchy, institutionalism, professionalism, and representative structures. They include larger professional NGOs, trade unions, and affiliated parties. Although some of these organizations, such as unions and parties, include mechanisms, such as elections or formal decisionmaking processes, to try to keep leaders accountable to their members or constituents, larger professional NGOs often lack these tools.[1]

This chapter considers the tensions involved in the World Social Forum's expression of the networking logic found in contemporary social movements. In what follows, we examine the WSF as an open space and consider how the multiple and often conflicting understandings of this space reflect fissures and tensions within the forum process itself.

The Cultural Politics of Networking

Since its first meeting in Porto Alegre, Brazil, in 2001, the WSF has reflected a networking logic prevalent within contemporary social movements and global justice movements in particular (Juris 2008). Facilitated by new information technologies, and inspired by earlier Zapatista solidarity activism and anti–free trade campaigns, global justice movements emerged through the rapid proliferation of decentralized network forms. New Social Movement (NSM) theorists have long argued that in contrast to the centralized, vertically integrated, working-class movements, newer feminist, ecological, and student movements are organized around flexible, dispersed, and horizontal networks (Cohen 1985). Indeed, Mario Diani (1995) defines social movements more generally as network formations. By promoting peer-to-peer communication and allowing for communication across space in real time, however, new information technologies have significantly enhanced the most radically decentralized network configurations, facilitating transnational coordination and communication.

Contemporary social movements are shaped by an emerging "cultural logic of networking." This series of broad guiding principles emerged from the logic of informational capitalism, or the lateral transference of information for profit-making, and these principles are internalized by activists as they develop networking practices (cf. Juris 2004a). They include (1) forging horizontal ties and connections among diverse, autonomous elements; (2) the free and open circulation of information; (3) collaboration through decentralized coordination and consensus decisionmaking; and (4) self-directed networking. Networking logics have given rise to what grassroots activists call a new way of doing politics. While the command-oriented logic of political parties and unions is based on recruiting new members, building unified strategies, political representation, and the struggle for hegemony, network politics involve the creation of inclusive spaces where diverse movements and collectives converge around common hallmarks, while preserving their autonomy. Rather than recruitment, the objective becomes horizontal expansion through articulating diverse movements within flexible structures that facilitate maximal coordination and communication.

Considerable evidence of this cultural logic of networking is found among organizations participating in the European Social Forum (ESF). About 80 percent of sampled organizations mention *collaboration and networking* with other national and transnational organizations as a main raison d'être of their groups. Many groups also emphasize the importance of collaboration with groups working on different issues but sharing the same values. Some groups even refer to themselves as *network organizations* (della Porta and Reiter 2006). Furthermore, research at the University of California–Riverside found that "networking" as a reason for attending the 2005 WSF was more common among nonlocal respondents (60 percent) than Brazilian respondents (26 percent) (Reese et al. 2006).

Although the tension between "horizontalism" and "verticalism" is apparent, the practice of horizontalism is also riddled with difficulties. Horizontalism is best understood as a guiding vision, not an empirical description. In practice, networking logics are never completely dominant, and they always exist in dynamic tension with other competing logics. Indeed, struggles within and among different movement networks shape how specific networks are produced, how they develop, and how they relate to others within broader social movement fields. Cultural struggles surrounding ideology (antineoliberal globalization vs. anticapitalism), strategies ("summit hopping" vs. sustained organizing),[2] tactics (violence vs. nonviolence), as well as organizational form (structure vs. nonstructure) and decisionmaking style (consensus vs. voting), have become enduring features of the global justice movement, including the social forums (Juris 2008).

Neither should horizontal networks be romanticized. Horizontal relations do not suggest the complete absence of hierarchy but rather the lack of formal hierarchical designs. This does not necessarily prevent, and it may even encourage, the formation of informal hierarchies, such as those based on interpersonal cliques or differences in skills and resources (Freeman 1974; cf. King 2004). What activists call horizontalism thus involves an attempt to build collective processes while managing internal struggles via decentralized coordination, open participation, and organizational transparency rather than representative structures and central command (Juris 2008). At the same time, the broadest convergence spaces (Routledge 2004), including the social forums, involve a complex mix of organizational forms. Yet networks have more generally emerged as a broader cultural ideal, a model of, and model for, new forms of directly democratic politics at local, regional, and global scales.

Social Forums as Open Space(s)

The network ideal is reflected within the WSF's organizational architecture through the concept of open space. What attracted so many movements to the WSF was its promise of a space for horizontal communication, reflecting the network principles characteristic of global justice movements more generally. The dominant model of open space within the WSF is an associational, that is, deliberative or discursive public space, and the other model is one of an agonistic public space. The first notion of the WSF as an ideal open space of deliberation and discussion is juxtaposed against a more critical notion of public space that emphasizes the reality of power, contestation, and conflict present in the WSF as in all social relations. After describing the emergence of the forum as an open space, in the sections that follow we consider each of these conceptions of open space at the WSF. We then explore the WSF as a contested space and a space of exclusion both within the forum and along its margins.

The WSF Charter of Principles defines it as "an open meeting place for reflective thinking, democratic debate of ideas, formulation of proposals, free exchange of experiences, and interlinking for effective action" (WSF 2001). Although the WSF provided an opportunity for the traditional left (verticals), including many reformists, Marxists, and Trotskyists, to claim a leadership role within an emerging global protest movement, radical network-based movements (horizontals) from Europe, North, and South America resisted a centralization of leadership. The WSF Charter of Principles provided guidelines for a permanent process that privileged decentralized network principles, allowing horizontals and verticals to coexist within the World Social Forum's open space.

The charter's reflection of the open space concept resists the adoption of programs of action by the WSF itself. It states: "The meetings of the WSF do not deliberate on behalf of the WSF as a body.... It does not constitute a locus of power to be disputed by the participants ... nor does it constitute the only option for interrelation and action by the organizations and movements that participate in it." However, this should be taken more as an ideal than actuality (cf. Waterman 2002) and, perhaps more importantly, as a reflection of a much broader horizontal networking ethic.

The foremost proponent of this concept of open space within the forum has been Francisco (Chico) Whitaker, one of the prime movers of the forum from its inception. Whitaker explains his view of the WSF-as-space in the following manner:

> A space has *no leader*. It is only a place, basically a *horizontal space*.... It is like a *square without an owner*.... [The WSF] is a space created to serve a common objective of all those who converge to the Forum, functioning horizontally as public space, without leaders or pyramids of power. The Forum is intended to serve as an incubator of ideas, a space in which movements to contest neoliberal globalization are created. (Whitaker 2004:113)

The central and innovative idea here is that the WSF is not an actor that develops its own programs or strategies, but rather it provides an infrastructure within which groups, movements, and networks of like mind can come together, share ideas and experiences, and build their own proposals or platforms for action. The forum thus helps actors come together across their differences, while facilitating the free and open flow of information. A survey of participants at the 2005 WSF, however, showed that respondents were fairly evenly split over the question of whether the forum should take positions on issues. Fifty-one percent of respondents believed that it should do so, rather than simply remaining an open space for discussion (Chase-Dunn et al. 2008).

Because the forum itself cannot issue declarations or make political decisions on behalf of all its members, it seems that there should be no reason to struggle for power. Moreover, as a public space, that is, a self-managed space of discursive production (cf. Warner 2002), there is no need for leaders or hierarchy. Yet many of the debates within and around the forums focus on the claims that it is flat, horizontal, and devoid of power relations. Indeed, the issue of whether the forum should remain a space or become an actor has been hotly contested. It may be that because the WSF and its founders tended to emphasize one form of public space over the other in the Charter of Principles, this has limited the forum's ability to deal with internal contestations that have become more pronounced.

Open Space as Deliberative Space

The dominant view of open space within the WSF is a deliberative, or discursive, public space. Jürgen Habermas, whose work is grounded in his theory of "communication action," is the primary proponent of deliberative theory of the public sphere (1992). Juxtaposing Habermas's work on the public sphere to the WSF Charter of Principles reveals important parallels. According to Habermas, contemporary societies are divided between the *system* and *lifeworld*. The system is composed of macrostructures dominated by money in the form of markets and by power in the form of the state and its institutions. The system is governed by instrumental rationality. The lifeworld, on the other hand, is governed by norms of communicative action, thus providing an insulated sphere for free and open communication among equals. Increasingly, thought Habermas, the system dominates the lifeworld, undermining the public sphere and democracy in the process.

Yet there was still hope for a revival of the public sphere and democracy as the lifeworld possessed certain features capable of resisting colonization by the political-economic system and its instrumental rationality. Communicative rationality is for Habermas a permanent form of opposition to the money and power of the system, giving rise to a form of political will formation based on reason and rational argumentation expressed through the process of "deliberative democracy." Habermas's concept of deliberative democracy was, writes Douglas Kellner (2000:12), "conceived as a process which cultivates rational moral subjects through reflection, argumentation, public reason and consensus." Moreover, these processes are based on the values of impartiality, equality, absence of coercion and openness (Mouffe 1999).

Most important to Habermas's interpretation is that a public sphere revived by deliberative democracy is divorced from the power, decisionmaking bodies, and apparatus of the state. As he notes, "discourses do not govern" (1992:452). In essence there is a disjuncture between speech and action, public discourse and power. "The public opinion that is worked up via democratic procedures into communicative power cannot 'rule' of itself, but can only point the use of administrative power in specific directions" (Habermas 1996:29).

The Habermasian discourse model of public space and democracy has considerable resonance in the theory and practice of the WSF. For example, the charter of the WSF makes it clear that the forum is not to be a space or locus of power. Rather, it should be a discursive space to generate ideas that others will take beyond the forum and act on in challenging neoliberalism and imperialism. In addition, the WSF as a public space is to be explicitly divorced from the power and administration of the state (see Chapter 3). Thus, there is an attempt to insulate the forum externally from "the system" and hierarchy. However, uncritically extending this notion to the forum's internal operations overstates the extent to which it is possible to escape system-level inequities and hierarchies.

In fact, a system and hierarchy persists within the forum itself. For instance, as Catherine Eschle and Bice Maiguascha (2005) document, feminists actively struggled to achieve greater visibility within forum events and greater influence over the WSF leadership and organization. They managed to gain representation on the International Council, increase the number of forum events focusing on feminist issues, and include issues of patriarchy in the thematic axes of WSF meetings. However, many feminists are still concerned with the lack of gender parity within the WSF and lack of attention to feminist issues within the main plenary sessions. In other words, the problematic claim that the lifeworld can exist autonomously from the system is reproduced within the forum through the notion of an open space devoid of hierarchy and power relations. Moreover, it is also possible to argue that the divorce between speech and action already noted in Habermas's theory is strongly reflected in the WSF through the idea of the forum as primarily a space for exchanging ideas and information. Others, somewhere, act. The World Social Forum deliberates.

The WSF as a deliberative public space nonetheless has a strong attraction for many of its participants. The WSF is, as Geoffrey Pleyers notes, "a public forum allowing for discussion and debate, strengthening thereby its members' ability to raise and accept arguments" (2004:510). Francesca Polletta (2002:9) speaks of this as a "developmental benefit" of participatory democracy. Empirical research by Donatella della Porta, Lorenzo Mosca, and others at the European Social Forum validates the ideal of deliberation as one instantiated in the practice of forum participants (della Porta and Mosca 2006). The fundamental documents of 244 organizations analyzed include the promotion of democratic values among their major objectives (della Porta and Reiter 2006). Many groups also articulate measures for promoting internal democracy within their organizations, although one finds a variety of conceptions of participatory democracy. Values such as *heterogeneity, equality, transparency, inclusiveness,* and *individual autonomy* are mentioned frequently in organizational documents, whereas representative values are mentioned by just 6 percent of the organizations included in the study. Despite these apparently widespread values of democracy, the forum itself risks becoming depoliticized to the extent that it fails to confront its own internal system of hierarchy and power (Teivainen 2004a).

Open Space as Agonistic Space

Engaging questions of power, Chantal Mouffe offers a competing conception of public space and democracy, one that provides an alternative means of understanding important realities of the WSF. Mouffe stresses "the need to acknowledge the dimension of power and antagonism and their ineradicable character" (1999:752), developing the concept of agonistic space. She argues that Habermas's notion of the public sphere eliminates conflict. A deliberative sphere and democracy in particular are based on the idea that rational argument should override power and politics. Yet, insists Mouffe, relations of power are constitutive of all social relations (1999:753) and necessarily affect the character of deliberations, often in ways that are invisible to participants. The challenge for democracy is thus to create forms of power that are supportive of its values.

Democratic societies must, Mouffe argues, accept dissent and create institutions through which it can be expressed. She stresses that the agonistic dynamic of pluralist democracy is not entirely divergent, but rather it is a "'mixed game' . . . in part collaborative and in part conflictual" (1999:756). Mouffe's understanding of an agonistic public sphere and radical pluralism had its precursor in Arendt's conception of politics and the public sphere. But Arendt also emphasized that public spaces can be multiple and do not necessarily have to surround the institutions of government. Publics spaces or, perhaps better said, counterpublics (Fraser 1992), can be created and exist elsewhere. Also, Arendt argued that vibrant public spaces also involve appearance, performance, and drama—cultural dimensions missing from the work of both Habermas and Mouffe.

In terms of the first point, Arendt argued that not only can new public spaces be created but politics and public spaces are not necessarily tied to any particular place, territory, or set of institutions. They can exist in a variety of social spaces and places. Arendt contended: "The *polis*, properly speaking, is not the city-state in its physical location, it is the organization of the people as it arises out of acting and speaking together for this purpose, no matter where they happen to be" (1958:198). Consequently, "wherever you go, you will be a polis" (Arendt 1958:198). Social forums are an excellent example of the emergence of public spaces outside state-centric territorially based institutions.[3] Many of the critiques within and around the forums are pushing the WSF toward a model of multiple open spaces, rather than a single open space, as we will see in Chapter 5. In terms of the second point the emphasis on our desire for distinction and recognition within public space underscores Arendt's view of public space as a political phenomenon, meant to be enacted in public as theater. Anyone who has attended a WSF can speak to the prominence of spectacle as one of its most attractive features. In this sense, the forum is not only a space for rational discourse, but it is also a space of performance that is very much embodied, both visually and emotionally compelling. Such performances reinforce solidarity among participants, creating the social glue that helps build common identities, and they encourage democratic practices of mutual listening, good-faith negotiation, and compromise.

Social Forums as Contested Terrains

The World Social Forum is also a contested terrain, both internally and externally. The subsequent section provides examples of how the forum embodies theories of public space, performance, and spectacle. From its opening march to its conclusion, the forum clearly is more than a Habermasian arena for rational discourse. As the forum has progressed there has been growing awareness of the limitations of the WSF as open space based narrowly on discursive premises. Increasingly the forum is being recognized as "a plural and contested space" (Osterweil 2004b: 187). As such, the WSF has its own antagonisms, differences, and tensions that have become self-evident in recent years as democratic contention turns inward.

Particularly contentious is the claim by Chico Whitaker that the forum is simply a space, one without a pyramidal politics or power relations. In fact, however, the WSF does have its pyramids of power. April Biccum, for example, contends that it would be naive to assume "that the open space is space without struggle, devoid of politics and power" (2005:127). Many of these struggles revolve around the organization of the forum in general and the role of the International Council (IC), the association of 150 nonelected organizations and intellectuals that decide where the global forums are held and how they are to be organized.

Many grassroots activists have criticized the IC, as well as local and regional organizing committees, for acting precisely as a closed space of representation and power, limited to certain prominent international organizations and networks with access to information and sufficient resources to travel. For example, during an IC meeting in Barcelona in April 2002, the direct action–oriented Movement for Global Resistance (MRG) was invited to become a member of the council. After a vigorous debate, MRG decided that it could not accept the offer because, as a horizontal network, MRG had no members and could not join a "representative" space such as the IC (Juris 2008). Indeed, this kind of political representation and decisionmaking by a relatively closed and, at least at the time, nontransparent body seemed to contradict the networking logic and open space ideal represented by the WSF itself. A delegate from MRG thus read the following declaration during the meeting:

> We would like to thank the Council for the membership invitation. . . . MRG is part of a new political culture involving network-based organizational forms, direct democracy, open participation, and direct action. A top-down process, involving a closed, nontransparent, nondemocratic, and highly institutional central committee will never attract collectives and networks searching for a new way of doing politics. This should be a space of participation, not representation. (quoted in Juris 2008)

Many IC members agreed with MRG's critique and vowed to make the IC a more open, transparent, and inclusive space, which to some extent has been accomplished (see Teivainen 2004a). In this sense, the IC itself is a complex, contested space. On the other hand, many others feel the WSF needs a centralized leadership committee based on a clear structure to make sure the process works. As Immanuel Wallerstein has argued, the WSF could not function without an organization, one that is hierarchical, has power, and makes decisions. The fact that an open space requires a relatively nonopen space to carry out basic organizational, logistical, and administrative functions is one of the central contradictions within the forum process, and one that has caused much debate (see, e.g., Teivainen 2006).

A similar debate developed around the European Social Forum. The European preparatory assembly (EPA) is the main decisional body of the ESF process, and it has some important differences from its world-level counterpart. The EPA is not presented as a (closed) council of delegates as in the case of the IC. The fact that it is called an assembly suggests a more participatory, open space logic. Indeed, anyone can participate in preparatory meetings, which are held in different European cities to facilitate participation from different countries. However, like the IC, EPA is criticized by grassroots activists as raising a de facto barrier to participation since only people with time and resources to travel can take active part in the organizational process at the European level. Moreover, information on these meetings is not always easily accessible and the transparency of agenda formation and decisionmaking has been questioned (Doerr 2005:19).

The conflict between networking and command logics, or vertical and horizontal organizations, was particularly acute within the ESF process. During the 2002 ESF in Florence many of the squatted social centers—empty buildings occupied by independent media groups, social rights activists, and political and cultural projects—were ambivalent toward the forum, criticizing the support given by local authorities, as well as the prevalence of large, bureaucratic organizations. In the first ESF, the shared experience of protest among Italian social movement organizations (especially the anti-G8 protest in Genoa in 2001) generated mutual trust between "verticals" and "horizontals." However, this relationship had become more tense during the second ESF. The development of autonomous spaces had been a (partial) solution to these tensions, but the conflict escalated during the organizing process for the 2004 European Social Forum in London. The rupture between older party or union organizations and newer, horizontal networks became particularly evident when grassroots groups criticized London's mayor Ken Livingstone, the Socialist Action faction, and other hierar-

chical organizations for dominating the organizing process leading up to the 2004 ESF. On the second day of the ESF, radicals
stormed a stage where the mayor was scheduled to speak to
publicly denounce what they perceived as the nondemocratic
and top-down way the forum had been organized (della Porta
2007; Dowling 2005; De Angelis 2005; Juris 2005a).

Space or Actor?

Another point of contention concerns whether the WSF is primarily a space, an actor, or both.[4] Whitaker, for example, argues
that the WSF cannot simultaneously be a space and an actor, an
implicit distinction between deliberation and the agonism of
contestation and struggle. Space, he insists, must be perfectly flat
or horizontal. A movement, he argues, implies organization,
objectives, strategies, programs, tasks, and leadership—in effect,
hierarchy. Space can thus facilitate the creation of actors, identities, and movements, but a movement cannot easily create a
space such as the WSF and also attract the diversity of movements the WSF currently does. Similarly, Gina Vargas writes that
a forum-as-actor notion denies the horizontal nature of the
process, even transforming the forum into a singular social
movement "acting in the name of a wide and generic global
movement in which inclusion is not guaranteed" (2004:230).

Others, such as Teivo Teivainen and Immanuel Wallerstein,
feel this position is too rigid. According to Teivainen, "it is possible to be an *arena* and an actor simultaneously" once "reasonably
transparent and democratic mechanisms have been established"
(2004b:126). Wallerstein argues for a middle ground whereby the
WSF would "allow space within its framework for the creation of
networks who take action" (Smith 2005). Indeed, the "assembly
of social movements" has taken on precisely this role within the
world and regional social forums, bringing together actors within
the forum to draft a final manifesto including a list of actions for

the coming year. Assembly organizers claim they are using, but not speaking on behalf of, the forum. But Chico Whittaker and others argue that many people do not understand the difference, and so the assembly is perceived as speaking for the WSF.

At the same time, a growing number of voices are calling for the forum to speak with a clearer and more united voice. For example, during the 2005 WSF in Porto Alegre a group of prominent intellectuals, the "Group of 19" (G19), drafted a series of proposals and presented them publicly as the "Consensus of Porto Alegre."[5] In response, many organizers downplayed the initiative as just one declaration among many (see Chapter 4). A larger group of intellectuals made a second attempt to forge a common set of principles and strategies at a meeting in Bamako on January 18, 2006, the day before the polycentric WSF began. Unlike the G19 intervention or the assembly of social movements, the event was clearly set apart from official activities, although the resulting "Bamako Appeal" was still widely perceived as coming from the WSF.[6] Many grassroots organizers and activists criticized the appeal's universalizing thrust and the closed process by which it had been organized. At the same time, the document seems to have struck a chord with many activists, with respect to both its content and broader goal of forging a common agenda. Indeed, the appeal has elicited dozens of endorsements and significant debate, even among those most committed to a deliberative open space ideal.

Using Open Space: The Dalits of India

Although controversies surround the open space concept and the WSF, for most participants these debates are less relevant to their work within the forums themselves. Many social movement networks participate in the social forums and utilize these spaces to their advantage. One social movement that has taken advantage of the forums has been the Dalits (formerly the "untouchables" of India), who have been negatively affected by neoliberal globalization in India, with its emphasis on privatization and reductions in public sector employment and services.

The Dalits quickly realized the advantages of the social forum and became engaged with the WSF at its inception in 2001, although they participated in limited numbers because of the high cost of travel. That changed in 2003 and 2004 when the Asian and World Social Forums were held in India, at Hyderabad and Mumbai respectively. There Dalits turned out in large numbers: 30,000 strong in Mumbai. They utilized the forums as a horizontal space, as a space of convergence, and as a space of performance and spectacle.

Since its inception, the WSF has demonstrated promise as a focal point for resistance to neoliberal globalization. In 2001, one prominent networked Dalit organization, the National Campaign on Dalit Human Rights (NCDHR), sent its general-secretary, Vincent Manoharan, to more closely investigate the WSF. There he found that it was "an open space, that . . . gives an opportunity to meet other similar people where you can build an alliance." Moreover the "WSF was totally against the globalization process. That is our focus" (Manoharan 2004). In brief, the objectives of the NCDHR were consistent with the WSF as an open space, a meeting place that civil society organizations opposed to neoliberal globalization can call their own. At these forums the Dalits sponsored a variety of sessions to discuss the impact of neoliberalism on the Dalits, including its intensification of casteism.

Yet, it would be a mistake to equate what occurs inside tents and buildings at a forum with the open exterior space itself. In this instance, there is within the Dalit movement a sense of public space much akin to Arendt's view of public space as a realm of appearance, performance, drama, and spectacle. As she observed, "no one in his right mind would ever put on a spectacle without being sure of having spectators to watch it" (1982:62). The Dalits announced their appearance at forum events with the relentless sounding of drums, songs, and music. Significantly, their use of drums today represents a repudiation of the historical relationship of the playing of drums and public space. Historically, in premodern times the Dalits were not permitted to walk into a public street during the cooler hours. Only in the scorching afternoon could the Dalits enter public spaces, and only then by beating drums to announce their arrival and allow dominant castes to vacate the spaces (Guru 2004:758). Today, Dalits have reappropriated the drumbeats as a symbol of pride, using them to claim their place in a public space of their creation and announce their rightful belonging.

Together, through drums, music, and song, which draw participants to their sessions and the use of these sessions to discuss, educate, and create bounds of solidarity with other social movement networks, the Dalits proclaimed that "another world is not possible without a global struggle against casteism in all its forms, both within and outside of India" (Conway 2004:372). The example of the Dalits underscores the centrality of culture to the politics and spaces of social forums where it has become a "key site for transformative political struggle" (Osterweil 2004a:499). Another example of the centrality of political culture to the social forum process has been the creation of autonomous spaces along the margins of the forum, to contest the "vertical" practices within the official forum while also making use of the space provided by the forum to practice horizontal forms of political engagement and expression.

The Cultural Politics of Autonomous Space

Grassroots activists have used the social forums as a platform for making visible the struggle between horizontal and vertical political practices. In this sense, spectacle and culture serve not only to reinforce collective identities but also to publicly express differences through conflict. We have already seen how horizontals engaged in confrontational direct action during the 2004 ESF in London, preventing Mayor Ken Livingstone from speaking. Yet forums have also provided a space for radicals to practice their own self-managed forms of political expression, developing an agenda, creating the physical space itself, planning actions, and engaging in political discussion in a more or less open and participatory way (though, of course, never without conflict).

For example, on the first day of the 2002 WSF, a group of direct action–oriented activists, radicals, and anarchists from the Intergalactika Laboratory of Disobedience (Caracol Intergaláctika), a grassroots space for horizontal encounter and exchange in the Forum Youth Camp, marched together with a Brazilian activist samba band to the Catholic University, where the official forum was being held. After arriving, the motley group climbed to the second floor and occupied the VIP room, throwing water into the air and chanting, "We are all VIPS, we are all VIPS!" WSF organizers were livid, but there would be no VIP room the following year. In this sense, the WSF provided a space for intervening within the larger forums through spectacle and cultural conflict.

The actions and discussions at Intergalactika provided a model for "autonomous spaces" at subsequent European and World Social Forums. For example, a declaration from grassroots activists at the Strasbourg No Border Camp in July 2002 stated with respect to the upcoming ESF in Florence:

> We agreed to launch the idea of constituting a concrete space for those of us who traditionally work with structures that are decentralized, horizontal, assembly-based, and anti-authoritarian; a space that would maintain its autonomy with respect to the "official" space of the ESF, but at the same time remain

> connected. . . . This would mean . . . having one foot outside
> and another inside the ESF. . . . This autonomous space should
> visibilize the diversity of the movement of movements, but
> also our irreconcilable differences. (quoted in Juris 2008)

This "one foot in, one foot out" model reflected a horizontal networking logic, challenging the vertical practices within the official WSF, while remaining connected to the forum. The tensions within the forum are continually being played out, forcing the social forums to evolve in response to actions taken by participants. Like the challenges at the London ESF, similar actions have also changed the shape of the social forums.

What began as a single project ultimately broke into multiple autonomous initiatives at the ESF in Florence, including Cobas Thematic Squares, the *Disobedientes* "No Work, No Shop" space, and Eur@ction Hub. After Florence, the autonomous space model caught on. At the 2003 WSF in Porto Alegre, grassroots activists organized several overlapping spaces, including a followup Hub project, the second Intergalactika, and a Z Magazine forum called "Life After Capitalism." Although emerging from distinct political contexts, autonomous spaces at the 2004 WSF in Mumbai were even larger, particularly as Indian grassroots movements were especially critical of the institutional NGOs leading the process. These spaces included Mumbai Resistance (organized by Maoist and Gandhian peasant movements) and the Peoples Movements Encounter II (led by the Federation of Agricultural Workers and Marginal Farmers Unions).

Autonomous spaces reached their fullest expression during the 2004 London ESF, where young radicals organized numerous projects, including Beyond ESF (a gathering of anti-authoritarian, anticapitalist struggles), Radical Theory Forum (a workshop exploring the links between theory and practice), Indymedia Center (a space for grassroots multimedia production, including a bar, computer lab, and cultural events), Labora-

tory of Insurrectionary Imagination (a forum for creative interventions and exchange, involving workshops, discussions, and
actions around the city), Mobile Carnival Forum (a project
using theater and music aboard a double-decker bus to address
issues such as peace, democracy, and neoliberalism), Solidarity
Village (vendors and stalls focusing on fair trade and alternative
economics), Women's Open Day (talks and films about women's
survival work), and Life Despite Capitalism (a two-day forum
regarding the "commons").[7]

Autonomous spaces have thus made use of the deliberative
space provided by the official forums to organize their own horizontal projects, while transforming the forum into an agonistic
space through both discursive debate and spectacular conflict. At
the same time, the model of the forum as a *multiplicity of networked spaces* rather than a singular, all-inclusive open space has
transformed the way the WSF is organized. For example, the
2005 WSF in Porto Alegre shifted from a central site at the
Catholic University toward a network of "World Social Territories" involving diverse thematic areas surrounding the youth
camp. The more grassroots, horizontal practices within the
youth camp were thus geographically situated at the center of
the forum this time, rather than along its margins. Similarly,
autonomous spaces at the 2004 ESF helped make the Athens
ESF (2006) more open, as plenary sessions privileging VIP lumi-
naries were eliminated in order to reduce internal struggle
between horizontals and verticals and to leave more space for
more horizontal activities such as workshops and seminars.

The Social Forum as a Space of Exclusion

The contention between the verticals and horizontals raises the
question of just how open the WSF and the ESF have been as a
space for debate in terms of those who attend and its focus.

Clearly the forum is not open to everyone. Indeed, the forum is a space of defined exclusions. According to its charter, only those adhering to its principles may attend. Those espousing violence, for instance, are excluded from participating. Also, debates continue about whether to allow for the inclusion of political parties and other elite actors. We consider the relationship of political parties more closely in the next chapter, along with an investigation of the broader question of who participates in the WSF process.

Chapter Three
WHO PARTICIPATES IN THE
WORLD SOCIAL FORUMS?

One of the most contentious debates about the World Social Forum (WSF) and its Charter of Principles centers on who should participate in the forum—exclusively civil society? Political parties? Governments? Many argue that civil society needs a space that is autonomous from the state and private sectors so that independent reflection and deliberation can take place. But social change requires that civil society influence other social actors, such as political parties and government officials, and therefore others believe that involving such actors in the WSF is essential. This chapter explores this critical debate. It begins by examining the characteristics of WSF participants and the extent to which the world's peoples are truly included in these meetings. It then considers the actual record of the relationships between the WSF and governments and political parties, which is far more messy and complicated than what is contained in the Charter of Principles.

Uneven Geographies of the WSF

Because it is widely recognized that developing countries are especially at risk of exploitation and domination, the world-level meetings of the World Social Forum have all been held in the global south (Porto Alegre, Brazil; Mumbai, India; and Nairobi, Kenya).[1] To better understand the political views and characteristics of WSF participants, the Transnational Social Movements Research Working Group at the University of California–Riverside collected a total of 639 surveys among participants at the 2005 WSF meeting.[2] To ensure the representation of a broad cross-section of WSF participants, surveys were collected in three

Map 3.1 Residences of participants in the 2005 WSF in Porto Alegre

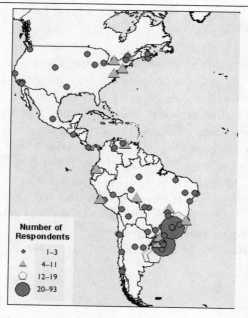

Number of Respondents
- 1–3
- 4–11
- 12–19
- 20–93

languages (English, Spanish, and Portuguese) and at a variety of events and venues, including the official registration line, a diverse array of thematic workshops, solidarity tents at multiple locations, outdoor music concerts, and the youth camp.

There is little doubt that an important degree of the prestige and legitimacy of the WSF derives from its effort to reach out and include "all the countries in the world." Official registration data indicate that participants came from 135 countries, but numbers of participants from these countries was uneven. Map 3.1 displays the 163 cities from which WSF participants came, based on the 520 responses in which this could be determined.

Obviously the "tyranny of distance," despite the slowly declining costs of long-distance transportation, continues to be a major factor in shaping the geographical nature of participation in the WSF. This can even be seen within South America.

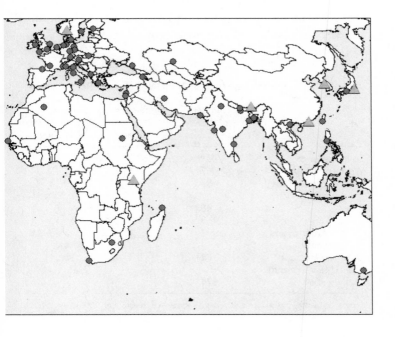

Seventy-nine percent of South American respondents, and 54 percent of all respondents, came from Brazil.[3] Table 3.1 shows the home region of the respondents of our survey.

Asia and Africa are the most seriously underrepresented world regions. Of course it is not just distance that skews participation. People from different regions also have very different financial resources and degrees of connectivity to transnational civil society. Table 3.2 shows the number and percentages of the 2005 WSF respondents from core, periphery, and semiperiphery regions, and compares these with percentages of the world's population in the countries in these categories, as reported by the U.S. Census Bureau, International Data Base. Core countries include the wealthiest of nations, such as the United States, most of Europe, and Japan; the semiperiphery represents middle-income countries such as Mexico, New Zealand, and several Latin American countries including Brazil; and the periphery is largely composed of the poorer countries of Asia, Africa, and Latin America with low levels of economic development.

Table 3.1   Region of Residence of 2005 WSF Survey Respondents

	Number of WSF Participants	Percentage of WSF Participants	Percentage of World Population in 2004
South America	439	69.0	6
Western Europe	67	10.5	12
North America (not including Mexico)	53	8.0	5
Asia	48	7.5	61
Africa	9	1.4	12
Central America and Caribbean	7	1.1	3
Oceania (Australia and New Zealand)	2	0.3	1
Total	625		

Source: University of California–Riverside survey (see Reese et al. 2006).

Table 3.2   Residence of Survey Respondents by World-System Zone

	Number of WSF Participants	Percentage of WSF Participants	Percentage of World Population
Core	125	19.6	13.3
Semiperiphery	451	70.6	54.6
Periphery	49	7.7	32.1
Total	625		

Source: University of California–Riverside survey (see Reese et al. 2006).

The core is not terribly overrepresented, but the periphery, which contains 32 percent of the world's population, is seriously underrepresented. That is one reason why Nairobi, Kenya, was selected as the site for the 2007 World Social Forum. The WSF and the forums generally have consciously sought to make these meetings as inclusive as possible, and the recognition that the location of meetings determines who can participate has motivated efforts to move the forum to different sites around the world.

In the European context, for instance, we notice a strong preoccupation with the need for inclusiveness. From their very beginnings, the ESF preparatory meetings included a working group called "expanding the network." One of the main concerns for the ESF has been the limited involvement of Eastern European civil society. Since it consciously seeks the construction of another Europe that vanquishes the barriers between Eastern and Western Europe, the ESF established a "solidarity fund" in 2003 to facilitate participation by Eastern Europeans. Although the Eastern European presence was limited in 2003, the Athens ESF in 2006 successfully involved more participants from Eastern European countries as well as from Turkey.

Characteristics of WSF Participants

The University of California–Riverside survey of participants of the 2005 WSF indicates that most, regardless of their home regions, are politically active. About 85 percent of respondents also indicated that they had protested at least once in the past year, while 31 percent indicated that they protested five or more times in the past year. While there was fairly balanced representation by gender, a higher share of those who traveled from outside of South America were men. Women from nations in the periphery were particularly underrepresented. That the WSF is a gender-integrated space is confirmed by various surveys. However, men seem to be disproportionately represented as speakers in WSF-sponsored events (Karides 2007).

A large number, 42 percent, of respondents were under 26 years. Most were also relatively privileged in terms of their race and class. White was the most common category that participants identified with in an open-ended question about race and ethnicity. However, changing the regional location of the WSF may change these demographics. WSF participants also tend to be well educated, and more than half, or 61 percent, of respondents had 16 years or more of formal education. Results from several other surveys conducted among WSF participants found similar patterns (Schönleitner 2003; IBASE 2006).[4]

Table 3.3 shows information about respondents' primary occupations. Nearly 70 percent of respondents were either students or employed in middle-class occupations (i.e., professionals, technicians, or artists). About 15 percent were professors or teachers, while one-third of respondents were students. Less than 10 percent of respondents could be considered part of the working class or peasantry. Only 6.7 percent were employed in semiskilled, nonprofessional service jobs, 1.1 percent were employed in farming, and 1.4 percent were employed in skilled, blue-collar jobs. No respondents identified as factory workers. Only 3.1 percent of respondents were unemployed or retired, a surprisingly low share given the high unemployment rates in South America. A majority of WSF participants are intellectuals and professionals.

The results of another extensive survey conducted in four languages among 1,000 participants of the WSF of 2005 by the Observatory of the Americas (of the University of Quebec in Montreal) confirm that the vast majority of respondents had a college or university degree and were associated with academic institutions. Of the respondents, 26.6 percent were students; teachers, 6.5 percent; university professors and university researchers, at 5.2 percent, also were represented. Employees in the private or public sector made up 9.5 percent of respondents; managers in the private or public sector, 4.7 percent; and independent professionals, 8.6 percent. This study showed a 1.1 percent participation rate of manual or factory workers but unemployed and retired workers were similarly underrepresented (Brunelle 2006).

Patterns of participation at the WSF of 2005 correspond to those in the European Social Forums as identified by the DEMOS Project. A large sector of the participants at the European Social Forums came from middle-class backgrounds. The

Table 3.3   Primary Occupation of Survey Respondents at the 2005 WSF

Primary Occupation	Number of WSF Participants	Percentage of WSF Participants
Professionals, technicians, and artists	230	36.0
Students	213	33.3
Activist/organizer	23	3.6
NGO worker (any capacity)	13	2.0
Semiskilled/nonprofessional white-collar workers	43	6.7
Skilled, blue-collar workers	9	1.4
Farming/agriculture	7	1.1
Self-employed, entrepreneurs, or managers	15	2.3
Unemployed	20	3.1
No answer or unclear answer	66	10.3
Total	639	

Source: University of California–Riverside survey (see Reese et al. 2006).

majority, 55 percent of participants surveyed at the first ESF, were students. Approximately 28 percent were employed, 8 percent self-employed, and 11 percent unemployed or marginally employed. Most participants, 88 percent, active in the labor market were employed in the service sector, almost evenly distributed between public and private enterprises. A large percentage, 15 percent, of activists at the ESF were teachers and university professors, especially those coming from France, 19 percent, and the UK, 26 percent.

These patterns reflect widespread inequalities in political participation, as more formally educated and middle-class people are more likely to vote and participate in other conventional political behaviors than those marginalized economically and educationally (see, e.g., Verba et al. 1995). But the relative absence of people of color, the working class, and other people who are excluded from the benefits of economic growth is clearly a problem that those concerned with democracy must confront. Democracy requires that all people have equal opportunities to participate, but if some people work too many hours or have no resources to assist them with child care and other household duties, they are effectively denied this democratic right. Economic barriers to broader participation in the forum have been a major concern of WSF participants, and solidarity funds have been used to help reduce these barriers. But our findings here remind us of the important contradiction in the economic order between the imperative for economic growth—which drives the ever-growing demands on workers' time and resources—and the need for institutions that have democratic legitimacy. The WSF's desire and demand for a greater role for civil society in economic decisionmaking cannot quickly overcome the structural barriers that the global economy places on workers. Nevertheless, efforts to bridge this economic divide in both the WSF and in national polities more generally should remain a priority of global justice advocates.

Gaining Representation: Ethnicity, Race, and Gender

The indigenous rights movements, communities of color, and women and feminist organizations are active participants in the forums. These groups and others vie for a more central role in the forum process, which they critique for emphasizing economic concerns over social issues in its events and thematic organization. We describe below examples of WSF participation from these groups as well as their criticisms of the social forums.

The Indigenous Rights Movement

With more than 100,000 people participating in the larger social forums, the WSF could assume the face of different parts of civil society depending on where an observer was positioned. At the 2003 World Social Forum in Porto Alegre, indigenous peoples struggled to make their presence and concerns felt, calling for the expanded participation of indigenous peoples in the forum. Nilo Cayuqueo, a Mapuche activist from southern Argentina, condemned the forum for excluding indigenous voices from the large plenary sessions.

Building on this momentum, indigenous peoples had a vastly expanded presence in the July 2004 Americas Social Forum (ASF) in Quito and the 2005 WSF in Porto Alegre. It was largely because of the strength of indigenous-based social movements and the power they have lent to antineoliberal struggles that the ASF was held in Ecuador. Meeting before the ASF, delegates at the Second Continental Summit of the Indigenous Peoples and Nationalities of Abya Yala debated a wide variety of issues, including land rights, self-determination, gender, and militarization. They drafted the Kito Declaration, which strongly condemned neoliberalism and the role of multinational corporations. During the ASF, Ecuador's indigenous movements organized a March for Life and against the Free Trade Area of the Americas (FTAA) and free trade agreements. While indigenous activists led the march, it reflected the broad diversity of issues and groups at the forum, including those of gender, sexuality, youth groups, leftist political parties, environmental groups, and peasant.

Half a year later, indigenous activists once again turned out in force for the 2005 Porto Alegre Forum to meet in a "Puxirum of Indigenous Arts and Knowledge." In the Brazilian Tupi-Guarani indigenous language, *Puxirum* means "a joining of efforts for a common goal." Their meeting ended with a declaration that "another world is possible, and we are part of that world" (http://ecuarunari.org/puxirum/declaracion.html). Having their own space within the forum, however, became a double-edged sword. Few of the 155,000 delegates in Porto Alegre managed to wander the several kilometers down the Guaiba riverfront to where the Puxirum was located at the edge of WSF activities. Over the course of the week, indigenous delegates increasingly left their space to join the forum's main activities. A year later, indigenous activists had a reduced presence at the polycentric WSF in Caracas.

Afro-Descendants

Afro-Latin Americans are another historically marginalized group that has used the WSF to forward their struggles and build links among themselves and with their counterparts. At the 2001 WSF in Porto Alegre, Afro-Brazilian organizations banded together to organize a tent featuring information regarding diverse struggles; stalls selling books, T-shirts, and handicrafts; and spaces for cultural performances, including collective dances and Capoeira (a Brazilian martial art). In addition, the Afro-Brazilian Committee and African Social Forum organized a high-profile panel addressing the growing demands for reparations for victims of colonialism and slavery, the need to produce accurate histories regarding Africa and the African diaspora, and the importance of confronting racist images of Africans in the mass media.

The following year activists organized the Quilombo Forum, a parallel space within the WSF dedicated to Afro-Brazilian struggles.[5] This featured cultural spaces, conferences and workshops, information stands, as well as book, clothing, and music stalls. One interesting activity involved a participatory workshop organized by the Thematic Working Group of Afro-descendents (NUTRAFO), which was designed to get participants to actually experience and confront racist attitudes. At the WSF in Porto Alegre in 2005, diverse networks and organizations created a conference on Afro-descendent communities' rights to housing and land, featuring testimonies from members of various Brazilian Quilombos and their counterparts from the Miami Workers Center.[6] Meanwhile, the International Youth Camp (IYC) featured various activities dedicated to cultural expression and political struggles among young Afro-Brazilians, including the Raizes (cultures of resistance) space and the Hip Hop dome.

Women, Feminists, and the Forums

Feminists and women's organizations use the forum as a space where they can initiate contacts, expand their organizational capacities, and strengthen transnational feminist networks (Alvarez et al. 2004). The WSF is also a space where tension within global feminism, such as the north-south division, the progressive and conservative perspective on control of women's bodies, and generational gaps can be addressed. For many the WSF is a space outside the UN structure where progressive women's movements can work in solidarity and also engage with the larger global justice movement.

Yet feminist and women's organizations engaging in the process of the WSF have leveled strong criticism at the sexist nature of the organization and, more fundamentally, on the absence of a feminist political economy as a framework for understanding global capitalism. Articulación Feminista Marcosur, an early participant in the WSF, argued that a "limited field of issues" takes precedence at the WSF (AFM 2005). This organization and others claim that rather than offering a plurality of views, economic analyses dominate the forum, perpetuating a monolithic vision of the methods by which to create a just society.

For many, gender and feminism made a strong presence in the 2004 WSF in Mumbai, India. One activist's reflections suggest that while the overall programming did not change, there was a stronger representation of women and the presentation of stark testimonies of gender oppression and firsthand accounts of gender violence. Another explains that the forum's inherent gender bias "somehow . . . was challenged and overtaken by women who decided to occupy more space than they had been given" (Vera-Zavala 2004).

Finally, while overall participation in the forums tends to be gender integrated, research on the ESFs suggests that "women without"—those with limited financial resources and those marginalized by their access to visas and border crossings—are less likely to be present in the forums and in the preparatory meetings of the forum (Doerr 2005).

WSF Participants' Affiliations with Movements, Organizations, and Parties

Rules from the WSF charter about who should participate in the WSF, and vocal debates among well-known activists and intellectuals regarding those matters, are one way of gauging how WSF participants view the role of political parties and civil society. Yet, it is also important to try to gauge how the hundreds of thousands of people attending the WSF understand the relationship between their party, organizational, and movement affiliations and their attendance at the WSF.

Table 3.4 shows the results from the University of California–Riverside survey about participants' organizational affiliations, whether they were attending the WSF on behalf of an organization, and whether they were planning to report back to an organization or social group about their experiences at the WSF. Consistent with concerns about the "NGOization of social movements," the largest share of respondents (39 percent) were affiliated with a nongovernmental organization (NGO). An almost equal share, 37 percent, of respondents belonged to a social movement organization (SMO), however, and a slightly greater share of respondents attended on behalf of, or planned to report back to, SMOs rather than NGOs. About 21 percent of respondents were affiliated with unions, although less than half of these respondents claimed they were attending the WSF on behalf of a union. Almost 17 percent of respondents were affiliated with political parties. Only 3 percent of respondents

Table 3.4 Organizational Affiliations of WSF Survey Respondents

	Percentage Affiliated With	Percentage Attending on Behalf Of	Percentage Reporting Back To
Nongovernmental organizations	38.7	17.2	28.5
Unions	21.3	8.6	10.8
Political parties	16.9	3.8	9.5
Social movement organizations	37.1	20.5	30.5
Government agencies	3.1	3.0	3.6
Other groups	10.1	7.5	23.6
No group	18.2	44.8	22.2

Source: University of California–Riverside survey (see Reese et al. 2006).

Note: Because participants sometimes have multiple organizational affiliations and commitments, the numbers in these columns do not add to 100 percent.

claimed to be affiliated with a government agency. About 10 percent claimed to be affiliated with another type of group than those just listed, such as a university, religious group, or media organization; more than twice this share of respondents (24 percent) claimed that they planned to report back to some other kind of group, including schools, religious groups, media outlets, friends, and family.

More than 93 percent of survey respondents claimed to be following the charter principle of not representing political parties or government agencies. Very small percentages of respondents claimed that they were attending the WSF on behalf of a political party or a government agency. Significantly, nearly one in ten respondents claimed that they were going to report back to a political party about their experience at the WSF, a practice that certainly would not be discouraged by the charter. These results suggest that although most WSF participants do not claim to be affiliated with political parties, a significant portion of WSF participants are actively involved in them and conventional politics more generally, and they view their participation in the WSF as relevant to the interests or activities of those groups. However, the Brazilian Institute of Social and Economic Analyses (IBASE 2006) found that 58.6 percent of respondents to their survey of participants in the 2005 WSF expressed distrust of political parties.

About 70 percent of WSF participants in this sample claimed that they were "actively involved" in at least one social movement, while about 40 percent were actively involved in three or more types of social movements. Table 3.5 examines the social movements in which WSF participants are active.[7] The most common social movements that respondents participated in involved human rights, environmental justice, alternative media/culture, global justice, or peace. More than one in ten respondents claimed they were active in the labor, fair trade, or women's movements. Although the majority of respondents in this sample expressed support for abolishing and replacing cap-

Table 3.5   Movement Affiliations of WSF Survey Respondents

Type of Social Movement	Percentage of Respondents "Actively Involved" In
Human rights/antiracism	25.2
Environmental	22.2
Alternative media/culture	20.8
Global justice	18.8
Peace/antiwar	17.7
Socialist	13.6
Labor	11.3
Fair trade	10.5
Feminist/women's	10.3
Health/HIV	8.1
Indigenous	7.5
Anticorporate	6.7
Food rights	5.9
National liberation	5.9
Queer/gay rights	5.8
Communist	5.0
Anarchist	3.1

Source: University of California–Riverside Survey (see Reese et al. 2006).

italism, most did not claim that they were currently part of ide-ologically based movements of the left (see Chapter 2). Whereas 14 percent identified as active in the socialist movement, only 5 percent claimed active involvement in the communist move-ment, and 3 percent in the anarchist movement. Some respon-dents claimed involvement in other kinds of social movements besides those listed in the survey questionnaire, including move-ments for children's rights, alternative education, students' rights, spiritual beliefs, and the solidarity economy.

Table 3.6 provides details about participants in the Euro-pean Social Forums, and we find that activists in political parties were also very much present there, where they constituted (according to a survey at the first ESF in Florence) about one-third of the participants, 34.6 percent. The same is true for trade unionists, 31.9 percent. Also, we found a strong presence of

Table 3.6 Movement Affiliations of European Social Forums Survey Respondents

Type of Organization	Percentage of All Respondents
Students	57.4
Social movements	52.7
Voluntary associations	51.2
Sports	50.9
Environment	43.1
NGOs	41.5
Parties	34.6
Immigrants	33.6
Social centers	32.2
Unions	31.9
Local committee	21.8
Women	21.7
Religious	19.2

Source: Survey taken by DEMOS at ESF in Florence, 2002.

Note: Number of valid responses: 2,475–2,503.

activists from various social movements (the women's movement, ecologists, student activists) at the ESFs, as well as multiple memberships in different types of organizations and groups. Party membership did not, however, indicate that participants have much trust in parties: only 20.4 percent of the participants in the first ESF trust parties a lot or enough (a percentage that remained constant also in the surveys on the ESFs in Paris and Athens).[8]

Logics of Exclusion: Should Parties and Governments Participate in the WSF?

Social movements and political parties can influence and build on each other's efforts. Thus, it is not surprising that, despite their formal exclusion from the WSF, representatives of political parties and governments have played important and visible roles within it as well as local and regional forums.[9] Some WSF participants are also beginning to explore issues surrounding the formation of global political parties. At present, the WSF seems unlikely to reconsider its decision to exclude political parties, military organizations, and governments from formal participation.

Formally, the Charter of Principles makes it clear that the WSF is an expression of civil society (see Appendix for full text). Its guiding Charter of Principles begins with the statement:

> The World Social Forum is an open meeting place for reflective thinking, democratic debate of ideas, formulation of proposals, free exchange of experiences and interlinking for effective action, by groups and movements of civil society that are opposed to neoliberalism and to domination of the world by capital and any form of imperialism, and are committed to building a planetary society directed towards fruitful relationships among Humankind and between it and the Earth.

For many activists in contemporary social movements, particularly those opposed to neoliberal globalization, the emphasis is on a new way of organizing, participating, and acting politically. As described in previous chapters, this new way of organizing is one based on horizontal relations embodied in network organizations, not on capturing power and exercising rule over others (Whitaker 2006:66). The vertical and pyramidal (i.e., bureaucratic) relations of governments and political parties are rejected as too authoritarian and controlling. The result is that parties are stigmatized as bearers of bad politics done by *professionals* interested in exploiting the global justice movement for electoral purposes and denying its political nature (della Porta et al. 2006:212). Both parties and the state machinery of public administration are seen as embodying a monopoly of knowledge. The perspective of the organized labor movement and the social democratic parties they supported was that the state under the control of the party was the prime agency of social change, the engineer of social justice. ...The role of the labor movement, the mass supporters, was to get the social engineers into place so that they deploy the instruments of state. Implementation of policy was seen as a technical matter, best left to the experts. (Wainwright 2003:11)

In this vision of politics, the electorate becomes an object of manipulation, a source of support for political parties to capture political power. For years after World War II, traditional parties of the left were successful in not only maintaining power, but implementing essential features of the welfare state. As we saw in Chapter 1, by the 1980s the place of the welfare state was being challenged by proponents of neoliberalism, as unions were weakened by the forces of economic globalization (see, e.g., Robinson 2004; Evans 1997). As activist journalist Naomi Klein observed, "All over the world, citizens have worked to elect social democratic and workers' parties, only to watch them plead impotence in the face of market forces and IMF dictates" (2002:21).

The result is that activists in the global justice movement are increasingly critical of public institutions. The protest is not only developing largely outside political parties but is also generating strong criticisms of representative democracy. Countering the depoliticization efforts of global elites described in Chapter 1, left-wing policies intersect with a rejection of the idea that politics is a specialized activity of a few professionals occupying elective posts in the public administration.

Indeed, demands for left-wing content and more participatory politics come together in the criticism aimed at the main political parties of the left. Leftist parties, although not part of the political landscape of the United States, are contenders for government positions throughout much of the globe, and they are increasingly powerful in Latin America. Many leftist parties, however, are seen as more concerned with managing administration and attaining and maintaining power than advancing progressive collective identities and a social agenda. Approaching the potential electorate through the media and perceiving it as predominantly centrist and moderate, leftist parties are critiqued for failing to support more participatory forms of democracy. In effect, they have contributed to the depoliticization of the electorate that has been essential to the expansion of neoliberal globalization (della Porta 2001). Mutual mistrust therefore grows between the parties who seek to replace activists with surveys and promotion campaigns, legitimizing representative rather than the direct democracy stressed by many activists.

Political parties accuse activists and organizations of being antipolitical or at best nonpolitical. Yet many activists respond with a concept of politics as an activity based on participation by everyone rather than a few professionals. Moreover, the essence of politics is considered the development of "demands" and "responses," namely, constructing identities rather than occupying power (della Porta et al. 2006:230–231). In response to military repression in Mexico, the Zapatistas have similarly turned from seeking political power to creating new forms of power outside of existing power structures.

Emerging from many movement activists is an alternative vision of politics, one that is based on direct participation and that rejects taking power in favor of a networked politics where activists embody in their practices the type of society they want to create within a democratic civil society. This practice of prefigurative politics opens new visions for building global democracy that the social forum process embodies and provides a space for (see Chapter 4).

Although parties and governments represent for many participants in the forums a type of outdated vertical politics, it is important not to overgeneralize activists' political views or to simplify their historical and dynamic relationships with political parties or with military organizations. In the European context, for instance, many countries have multiparty systems that include radical, left-wing political parties. Some of these parties are perceived by social movements as possible allies, but the fear of co-optation is always present in discussions taking place among social movement activists and organizations. In order to face the problem of the status of political parties toward the social forum process, the preparatory assemblies of the first ESF in Florence, Italy, in 2002 discussed this issue. A subsequent meeting in Vienna in May 2002 drew up several guidelines that make the ESF quite accessible to political parties but limit the "visible moments" of parties as an entity in their own right. Specifically, party representatives are allowed to be part of national delegations representing national social movements while party leaders, cadres, and members can directly register to the forums. Limits to political parties were abolished after the third European Social Forum (in London, 2004) since the limits rapidly became loci of power struggles among big, resourceful, and vertical organizations.

Despite the challenges of formally engaging more powerful political actors, evidence from the European Social Forums shows that such movement-party engagement can affect social change. For instance, the 2001 demonstrations against the G8 meeting in Genoa exposed the involvement of local and national social democratic parties in the privatization of public utilities and increasing labor market flexibility—that is, decreasing the number of secure, regulated jobs. European social democratic parties, although with some national variance, argued that neoliberal globalization strategies would ultimately benefit Europe, despite what were argued to be short-term inequalities. By exposing the social democrats' actions and rhetoric, the European global justice movement enriched the debates about globalization and global activism within the left-wing political parties in various European countries. It was especially through the organizational process of the ESF that a part of the institutional left began to engage with newer social movements. In short, the participation of parties on the left within the ESF process has forced social democratic parties to adopt a more critical stance toward globalization as they face new electoral competition from left-leaning and green parties.

Depending on the political context, parties can have very different roles and relationships within the social forum process. In many South American countries, including Argentina, Brazil, Venezuela, Chile, Uruguay, and Bolivia, leftist parties are on the rise, and many activists see them as vehicles for social change, even though these activists might be critical of the parties' policies. For many, the much debated shift to the left is part and parcel of the WSF process itself, but at the same time represents a challenge to WSF autonomy.

In Nepal and parts of the Philippines, Maoist Communist Party activists have sought to seize power through guerrilla warfare rather than the ballot. There, many anti-imperialist activists see party and movement activities as closely interconnected and consider violence a political tactic—despite Whitaker's and others' rejection of violence. As discussed in Chapter 2, rules prohibiting representatives of military organizations, while helping to safeguard against efforts to police the forum, limit the breadth of forum debates by discouraging consideration of the voices of such militant, modern-day revolutionaries.

What Experience of the Forum Tells Us

Despite the best intentions of those who believe in a new, horizontal politics of participation, one that excludes parties and governments, the practice of the forum tells a different story. As the European case (of allowing political parties to participate in the ESF) demonstrates, boundaries between governments, political parties, and the forum are fluid. Indeed, from the first WSF there has been a close linkage among the three. With the exception of the Mumbai WSF in 2004 and in Nairobi in 2007, all major social forums have had support from governments with close links to political parties. Clearly, Porto Alegre was host to the first WSF because both municipal and state governments were willing to extend material and human resource support (Teivainen 2004b).

The presence and support of governments and political parties have been noticeable and have led to pronounced tensions within the forum. Indeed, as the WSF grew, the necessity of its reliance on traditional state structures became increasingly apparent. Along with the European examples provided above, the relationship among parties, governments, and the forum can be illustrated by comparing the participation of President Luiz Inácio Lula da Silva of Brazil in 2003 with the participation of President Hugo Chavez of Venezuela in 2005.

The largest event of the 2003 forum and a highlight for many was a brief appearance by Lula. As it was a meeting of civil society, politicians acting as representatives of a political party were explicitly excluded from the forum, but nevertheless Lula was an overwhelming presence—both as an early instigator of the forum and as Brazil's newly elected, popular leftist president. In a talk to more than 100,000 people at the outdoor amphitheater Pôr-do-Sol on the edge of the forum's activities, Lula announced that he was leaving for the World Economic Forum "to demonstrate that another world is possible; Davos must listen to Porto Alegre." He said that "the world does not want war; it wants peace and understanding." After only three years, the WSF had "constructed the most extraordinary civil society experience anywhere in the world." Lula's presence at the WSF underscored a tension between civil society and political parties that has long characterized social movement organizing (Becker 2003).

On the other hand, Hugo Chavez was a less than welcome visitor to the 2003 forum. As the president of Venezuela, Chavez could not formally participate. Instead, he had to meet with his supporters in a small auditorium away from the main events. The contrast with the forum's treatment of the Brazilian president was notable. While he was not on the formal program, organizers engaged in intellectual gymnastics to open a space for the popular Lula, who appeared to represent the best hopes and aspirations of the Latin American left. The same courtesy was not extended to Chavez.

However, by 2005 much had changed. Both presidents again came to Porto Alegre and their receptions were radically different—from each other as well as from two years earlier. On the second day of the six-day meeting, Lula headlined an event at the Gigantinho stadium packed with 15,000 people—one of the largest meetings of the forum but small compared with the estimated 100,000 people who had turned out to cheer him in 2003. The purported purpose of the meeting was to launch the Global Call to Action Against Poverty (see www.whiteband.org). The real purpose, however, seemed to be an attempt to shore up his support from civil society, which had become skeptical of his increasingly neoliberal policies. The spectacle turned into a shouting match between supporters sporting red "100 percent Lula" T-shirts and a radical left opposition that wanted to hold Lula to the Workers' Party (PT) platform, which rejected the interference of international institutions in Brazil's economy. Lula also sent some of his ministers to participate in various workshops during the WSF, and their interventions indicated openness to working more closely with civil society, but we cannot confirm if the intent was to actually bring ideas, contacts, and information from the WSF into the formal policy process.

On the second to last day, Chavez packed Gigantinho stadium to overflowing with his own show. This event was much larger and more significant than his meeting two years earlier.

"I'm not here as president," Chavez noted in a seeming acknowledgment of the forum's roots as a movement of civil society. "I'm Hugo. The presidency is just a crappy job I've been assigned. I'm really just a peasant, a soldier, a man committed to the struggle for a better world." Chavez engaged in his characteristic strong anti-imperialist discourse. He cast his message as "the South stopping the destruction of the Bush doctrine" (Becker 2005). Chavez strongly condemned neoliberalism and imperialism for taking resources away from the poor to benefit the wealthy.

Chavez consciously contrasted his reception, his political positions, and the situation in Venezuela with those of his last visit in 2003. He also spoke of his dream for a unified Latin America, now made more real with leftist presidents Nestor Kirchner and Tabaré Vasquez in power in Argentina and Uruguay. Chavez noted that the WSF was the most important political event in the world. Venezuelans, he noted, "are here to learn from other experiments." The WSF provided a solid platform for debate of the issues that would lead to advances in the Venezuelan process. While Lula was lauded for his participation in the 2003 forum, by 2005 he was loudly criticized and Chavez became the most prominent politician that year.

Yet the extensive involvement of Chavez's government in the logistics of the 2006 polycentric forum in Caracas, Venezuela, received a great deal of criticism. Voices of dissension were evident throughout the panels as many participants were concerned with what seemed to be a transgression of WSF principles. In particular, the Chavez government's involvement in building the International Youth Camp (IYC), a location for young persons and those not staying at hotels to camp and congregate, was widely criticized as failing to meet the accessibility and provisions of previous forums.

Many activists have been rethinking the relationship between social movements and political parties. Thomas Ponniah from the Network Institute for Global Democratization noted that social movements, unlike parties, were able to mobilize the greatest global demonstration in history against the war in the Iraq. Yet social movements are not able to act like governments, which were able to pull their troops out of Iraq as in the case of Spain. He calls for a new relationship between the two (cited in Becker 2007).

Other activists also argue for a closer relationship between social movements and political parties. According to Chris Nineham and Alex Callinicos, "it was a mistake to impose a ban on parties, since political organizations are inextricably intermingled with social movements and articulate different strategies and visions that are a legitimate contribution to the debates that take place in the social forum" (2005). Bernard Cassen, a promoter of the WSF, argues pointedly: "We can no longer afford the luxury of preserving a wall between elected representatives and social movements if they share the same global objectives of resisting neoliberalism. With due respect for the autonomy of the parties involved, such wide cooperation should become a central objective of the Forums" (2006:83). As a pragmatist and reformer, Cassen is among those who maintain that parties and governments are vehicles to challenging, if not rolling back, neoliberal globalization.

Is the WSF a Site for Global Party Formation?

Bringing together activists from many movements and countries, the WSF provides a strategic site for forming new kinds of political organizations. As we have discussed, many WSF participants, like social activists more generally, express a desire for horizontal organizational structures rather than hierarchical ones. Many who have grown weary of the emptiness of representational forms of democracy, or the contradictions and broken promises of so-called leftist parties, are also calling for participatory forms of democracy. Such views have led to a certain degree of skepticism among many social activists around the world about the liberating potential of representative democracy and political parties. Surveys and interviews with activists in the global justice movement in Europe revealed that many viewed political parties as operating in a top-down fashion and driven by unaccountable politicians whose own desire to maintain power and legitimacy conflicts with the interests of their constituents (della Porta et al. 2006).

Because of the negative connotations associated with political parties, some activists and intellectuals seeking to challenge the power of global governance institutions are calling for the creation and spread of new kinds of political agency, such as "political cooperatives" or "political instruments." Yet, political parties can take multiple forms and it is important not to reproduce false dichotomies between civil society organizations and parties given the historically variable and complex interrelationships between them (Patomaki and Teivainen 2006). Indeed, while many European social activists are dismissing the importance of electoral politics, many activists in other parts of the world, especially in South America, have actively contributed to the rise of socialist parties, and worked both inside and outside of electoral and legislative arenas to pursue social change. Nor should we assume that all parties must necessarily operate within existing national boundaries or in a top-down, hierarchical fashion. Horizontally organized groups who are coordinating their political activities transnationally can be thought of as global networks, or even as world parties.

The activist-scholars of the Network Institute for Global Democratization in Tampere, Finland, have recently examined the topic of world party formation in historical perspective (Sehm-Potamaki and Ulvila 2006). Efforts by local and national groups to come together—in transnational and international coalitions and organizations—are certainly not new. Since the nineteenth century, nonelites have organized world parties. In the twentieth century these came to be structured as federations of nationally constituted member organizations, though earlier world party organizational forms were more transnational than international. Indeed, transnational and international political alliances and organizations have played important roles within world revolutions for centuries (Arrighi, Hopkins, and Wallerstein 1989; Boswell and Chase-Dunn 2000). The contemporary efforts by activists to overcome cultural differences; deal with potential and actual contradictory interests among workers, women, environmentalists, consumers, and indigenous peoples; and solve other problems of the north and the south need to be informed by both the failures and the successes of these earlier struggles.

Participants in the WSF process appear to be highly ambivalent about the twofold nature of the forums as open space arenas of discourse versus an organized movement of movements. But the forum process does not preclude subgroups from organizing new political instruments, and there seems to be an increasing tendency for more structured and coordinated global initiatives to emerge from the forum process. Indeed, in recent social forum meetings, meetings of social movements and other groups have issued calls for action and other political statements (see Chapter 2). These responses to the perceived limitations within the existing WSF structure are potential catalysts to the creation of new forms of politics that are more appropriate to the needs of an increasingly integrated world. Events like the massive global day of action against the war in Iraq (which was generated by social movements at the ESF and subsequently the WSF meetings in Porto Alegre) and the dissemination of the Bamako Appeal discussed in Chapter 2 reveal a desire on the part of WSF participants to find new ways of acting together across national borders. These actions, while not formally considered part of a WSF platform, reflect attempts to demand mechanisms of democratic participation in a world political order that denies these. Creating democratic mechanisms of accountability through which WSF participants can engage in global collective action and move toward greater political unity while respecting diversity remains an absolutely vital political task.

Although some scholars and activists contend that global democracy requires the abolition of global governance institutions, others call for restructuring them, and possibly even forming a true world government in order to regulate the international economy so that it better responds to public needs (e.g., see Patomaki and Teivainen 2004; Cavanagh and Mander 2004; Held and McGrew 2002; Boswell and Chase-Dunn 2000). While there have been a number of criticisms made of the WSF by activists, many see the WSF as an important instrument for preparing the public to participate actively within, and influence the decisions of, such institutions.[10] For example, Smith (2004b:420) argues that the WSF is a "foundation for a more democratic global polity," since it enables citizens of many countries to develop shared values and preferences, to refine their analyses and strategies, and to improve their skills at transnational dialogue. Heikki Patomaki and Teivo Teivainen (2004:151) suggest that the WSF "forms a loosely defined party of opinion" from which global parties could emerge and wield influence on world politics. Desire to create a more democratic global political economy could lead to greater support for global party formation at the WSF, despite many activists' reservations about political parties.

Conclusion

Who participates in the WSF process is important, given that the process itself aims to expand participation in global politics and to reduce the social and economic exclusion that our existing political and economic structures have produced. But while

WSF participants seek to reduce inequalities, they have not fully overcome the structural challenges in this regard. The realities of geographic economic inequality limit the global representativeness of WSF participants, and those closest to the sites of social forums and those with greater access to education and financial resources are, not surprisingly, overrepresented in the social forums. Those most in need of the kinds of economic and political changes advocated by the global justice movement, ironically, are least able to bring their own voices to WSF spaces. However, those active in shaping the WSF process have demonstrated a strong commitment to enhancing the inclusiveness of the WSF, and we expect that the characteristics of forum participants will change over time, as new forms of direct participation and new strategies of inclusiveness are enacted in the WSF process.

The tensions surrounding the role of political parties in the WSF remain and contribute to the continuous self-reflection that has become part of the forum process, helping ensure that no two social forums will ever be alike. As a contingent and mutable space, the WSF and related forums will both reflect the local politics and society where they are held and lead to reevaluations of the status of political parties and governments in these spaces. Whether these may one day become formal participants or whether WSF participants will be content to live with this ambiguity remains to be seen.

Chapter Four
REFORMISM OR RADICAL CHANGE: WHAT DO WORLD SOCIAL FORUM PARTICIPANTS WANT?

A s we have seen in previous chapters, the World Social Forum (WSF) is an extremely complex process made up of a staggering diversity of actors, each with their own background, history, context, and goals. Any attempt to characterize the political vision of forum participants as a whole is thus quixotic at best, and at worst violates the spirit of the WSF Charter. As is explained in Chapter 2, the charter states that no one can speak in the name of the forum or its participants. That said, the movements and networks that attend the world and regional forums do have a clear set of ideas about what another world would look like.

Despite disagreement on many issues, most participants share certain fundamental points in common, most notably the desire to help people take back democratic control over their daily lives. Whether this should happen through the destruction of the capitalist system, as radicals would argue, or through regulating the global economy, as reformists would contend, is a matter of intense debate. Likewise, forum participants are also divided on whether to negotiate with existing global political and financial institutions or to radically restructure them along more democratic lines. At the same time, many participants would argue that it is possible to work toward long-term structural change, while enacting concrete reforms along the way that benefit people struggling right here and now. Indeed, such debates are what make the forum such a lively and captivating process.

This chapter attempts to provide a snapshot of the differences in political visions and goals among forum participants, as well as some of the concrete proposals and alternatives they are developing. Rather than characterizing the forum as a whole, however, it introduces the major sectors that take part in the forum process and describes their views and objectives. We also introduce some of the major ideological debates and fault lines within and around the forum. This chapter makes certain generalizations and depends on categories that may not be as fixed as presented, so it is important to remember that there is a great deal of diversity within each of the political sectors. In what follows, we begin by outlining the primary movement sectors that participate in the forum process, including their social composition and political beliefs. The next section further explores the major political and ideological tensions running through the forum process, making reference to interview data collected during the 2005 WSF in Porto Alegre. Then, we examine some of the concrete goals and proposals promoted by "radicals" and "reformists," within and along the margins of the forum. Finally, the chapter concludes by considering how these issues might play out within the U.S. context.

Movement Sectors

The social forums are characterized by a diversity of movement actors, each with their own particular social composition, ideological visions, and political goals. Before considering specific proposals and views among forum participants, it might be helpful to briefly delineate these sectors to provide a wider context. We divide forum participants into four political sectors: institutional movements, traditional leftists, network-based movements, and autonomous movements (Juris 2008). These categories help provide a road map, but in practice the distinctions we make are more fluid and dynamic than presented here. Participants move among sectors or engage with multiple sectors simultaneously depending on which organization or network they participate in. The remainder of this section outlines each of these sectors, focusing on their social and ideological characteristics.

Institutional Actors

Institutional actors operate within formal democratic structures, aiming to establish social democracy or socialism at the national or global level. This sector primarily involves political parties, unions, and large NGOs, which are generally reformist in political orientation, vertically structured, and characterized by representative forms of participation, including elected leaders, voting, and membership. Formal organizations (again to generalize) tend to involve older participants and are more likely to have members with stable jobs and families than their grassroots counterparts. The members of parties and unions are mostly working-class and their racial background varies by country. Given their reformist political orientation, institutional actors tend to promote concrete political and economic reforms not only through protests such as the marches that take place during the forum but also through formal participation in electoral politics. These include canceling the foreign debt, democratizing the World Bank and WTO, or enacting a small tax on global financial transactions (Tobin Tax). According to this view, the forum process generates concrete policy proposals and serves as a political tool to promote their implementation.

Traditional Leftists

This sector includes various tendencies on the radical left, including traditional Marxists and Trotskyists, who identify as anticapitalist, but tend to organize within vertical organizations where elected leaders rather than a wider range of members make organizational decisions (see Chapter 2). Some work within leftist parties and trade unions, NGOs, or grassroots networks, such as the Association for the Taxation of Financial Transactions for the Aid of Citizens (ATTAC), forming a radical bloc within mainstream leftist institutions, while others prefer open assemblies and tend to work through grassroots social movements, but with the goal of recruiting members or moving the discourse in a more radical direction. In many countries, the social backgrounds of traditional leftists are often similar to institutional actors. However, traditional leftists are resolutely anticapitalist, although unlike network-based or autonomous movements they are more influenced by state-centered revolutionary strategies. In this sense, their ultimate goal is to abolish capitalism by taking control of the state. At the same time, moderates sometimes favor concrete reforms as long as they are steps toward deeper structural change.

Network-Based Movements

This sector involves grassroots activists associated with decentralized, direct action–oriented networks, including the former Direct Action Network (DAN) in the United States, the UK-based Reclaim the Streets, the Italian Disobbedienti, or the ex-Movement for Global Resistance (MRG) in Barcelona, as well

REFORMISM OR RADICAL CHANGE? 83

as Peoples Global Action (PGA) on a global scale. These networks are often temporary, lasting a few months to several years,
and are critical of vertical forms of organizing, including formal
institutions and traditional leftists. Influenced by a horizontal
networking logic, network-based movements stress direct
democracy, autonomy, and global coordination among local
struggles within diffuse structures. They resist formal organizational structures and leadership roles. Some participate actively
in the WSFs, while others participate within various
autonomous spaces during the forums (see Chapter 2).

At the same time, network-based movements are often
allied with popular movements in both the global north and
south that have a strong base among poor people and people of
color. In terms of ideology, network-based actors have a radical
anticapitalist vision, but unlike traditional leftists, they are committed to decentralized, participatory forms of organizing.
Rather than state-centered strategies, the goal is thus to create
spaces of democratic self-organization through horizontal networking. Indeed, political visions are often expressed as much
through process as political discourse. At the same time, most
activists within radical network-based movements would support reforms as a step toward more fundamental change.

Autonomous Movements

Autonomous movements, including militant squatters (radical
activists who occupy abandoned buildings and create self-managed social centers) in the north and certain indigenous and poor
people's movements, such as the Brazilian Landless Workers
(MST), the Karnataka State Workers in India (KRSS), the Zapatistas in southern Mexico, or the U.S.-based Immokolee Workers and Kensington Welfare Rights Union, mainly emphasize
local struggles (Starr and Adams 2004). These movements also

engage in transnational networking, but their primary focus is local self-management. Autonomous movements tend to be staunchly anticapitalist, assuming a posture of direct confrontation and promoting solutions beyond the market and state. Some militant autonomists have a critical perspective toward global justice movements. At the same time, many participate in alternative anarchist or anticapitalist platforms during the social forums, or sometimes within autonomous spaces together with their counterparts from network-based movements (Juris 2005a). In addition to radically confronting the system through direct action, autonomous movements stress alternatives based on self-management and directly democratic decisionmaking. Projects include squatting land and abandoned buildings, grassroots food production, alternative currency systems, and creating horizontal networks of exchange (Starr 2005).

Political and Ideological Tensions Within the Forum

Given the diversity of political and ideological visions reflected in the movement sectors outlined above, the WSF process is characterized by significant political tensions and ideological fault lines. The vast majority of those who attend the WSF identify as left-of-center in political orientation. A survey conducted by Fundação Perseu Abramo of WSF participants of the 2001 meeting in Porto Alegre, Brazil, for example, found that 81 percent of their respondents identified as leftists, extreme leftists, or center leftists, with 60 percent identifying as part of the left (Schönleitner 2003:129). Similarly, the Brazilian Institute of Social and Economic Analyses (IBASE 2006) found that 80 percent of respondents surveyed at the 2005 WSF in Porto Alegre identified as left or center-left, with 60 percent identifying as leftists. However, within the leftist identity, forum participants lean toward either "reformist" or "radical" perspectives. Reformists generally think that the capitalist system can be reformed while radicals think it should be abolished and replaced with something else. Institutional actors can be generally characterized as reformers, while traditional leftists, network-based movements, and autonomous movements tend to hold radical views. As stated earlier, traditional leftists and network-based movements are more open to reforms than autonomous movements, as long as these are viewed as a step toward radical change. The remainder of this section describes some of the major political and ideological fault lines within the WSF and provides some data regarding the percentage of participants who hold more reformist rather than radical views.

Reform or Revolution

As mentioned above, one of the major tensions running through the social forum process involves whether the world capitalist system should be reformed or abolished. Reformers believe that the negative effects of corporate globalization can be ameliorated by democratizing global political and economic institutions and by implementing specific political and economic reforms. Radicals, on the other hand, believe that current global trends, including growing poverty and inequality, increasing precariousness, and deteriorating environmental conditions, are structural effects of the global capitalist system itself and, therefore, global capitalism should be abolished. On the whole, the majority of WSF participants seem to support radical change. For example, results from the 2005 University of California–Riverside survey indicate that a majority of, or 54 percent of, all respondents (and 58 percent of those who answered the question) expressed the belief that capitalism should be abolished and replaced with a better system, rather than reformed. Moreover, researchers found that,

Table 4.1   Responses to the question: Do you think we need to reform capitalism or abolish it?

Response	Valid Percentage
Reform it	42
Abolish it and replace it with a better system	58
Chose both answers	1

Source: University of California–Riverside survey (see Reese et al. 2006)

Note: Number of responses: 548.

controlling for the effects of other factors, WSF participants who were young in the 1960s, and who were affiliated with self-funded political organizations, unions, and social movement organizations, were significantly more likely than participants without such affiliations to hold anticapitalist views and to favor the abolition or replacement of the IMF and WTO (Reese et al. 2006).[1]

Democratize Versus Abolish Global Financial and Political Institutions

Another important fault line within the social forum process and a more specific indicator of reformist versus radical views involves the question of whether global financial and political institutions should be reformed or abolished. Reformists argue that the problem is not necessarily capitalism per se, but rather corporate globalization or neoliberalism. Global institutions such as the World Bank, International Monetary Fund, and World Trade Organization are currently promoting free market principles, including privatization, fiscal austerity, low interest rates, export-led production, reduced trade barriers, cuts in basic subsidies, and other measures associated with the "Washington Consensus," or neoliberalism. These policies should be changed to allow governments to take on a greater role within national and regional economies through economic redistribution, strategic tariffs, and subsidies for key local industries. Rather than promoting capital's expansion, global institutions could play a different role within the global economy through measures such as taxing transnational financial transactions, outlawing fiscal paradises such as offshore banks where elites hold their savings to avoid taxation, as well as creating and enforcing minimum labor and environmental standards. In other words, a reformed World Bank, IMF, and WTO would provide an alternative institutional arrangement for managing and regulating the global economy. At the same time, reformists argue that these institutions should be democratized and made more accountable to their constituents within local governments and communities.

Radicals, on the other hand, argue that global political and economic institutions are a critical part of the global capitalist system and should thus be abandoned along with the system itself. Some, including many autonomous movements, maintain that all global institutions are harmful, and that we need alternative institutions that are much closer to the people whose lives they most affect. Others defend the need for global institutions, but argue that reforming the World Bank, IMF, and WTO would be impossible. For many, the United Nations could provide an alternative institutional arrangement that is more democratic and more responsive to the needs of local governments and communities around the world. Attempting to move beyond the reform-versus-abolish debate, some networks have called for more radical restructuring. In this sense, current global political and economic institutions would be abolished and replaced with new kinds of thoroughly democratized institutions.

In the views of WSF participants, there seems to be more taste for abolishing current global political and economic institutions than reforming them. The above-mentioned survey at the 2005 WSF in Porto Alegre found that 84 percent of respondents

**Table 4.2   Responses to the question: In the long run, what do
you think should be done about the existing
international financial and trade institutions such
as the IMF and the WTO?**

Response	Valid Percentage
Negotiate with them	13
Abolish them	25
Abolish and replace them	59
Chose more than one answer	3

Source: University of California–Riverside survey (see Reese et al. 2006)

Note: Number of responses: 567.

preferred to abolish existing institutions. Of these, 25 percent
wanted to get rid of these institutions, while 59 percent wanted
to replace them with more democratic alternatives. By contrast,
only 13 percent supported negotiation with global institutions.
Similarly, IBASE (2006) found that more than 80 percent of
respondents in 2005 expressed "distrust" of a number of leading
institutions of global capitalism: the IMF, WTO, banks, and international companies. These results suggest that even among
reformists at the WSF there is a widespread sense that institutions such as the World Bank and IMF should be abolished.
However, whereas reformists would seek reforms from existing
global governance institutions, radicals are divided on whether
or not to replace them. Traditional leftists are more likely to support alternative global institutions, while network-based and
autonomous movements are critical of all such institutional
arrangements.

World Government or Local Self-Management

The issue of whether current global political and economic
institutions should be replaced by alternative institutions sug-

gests a wider ideological tension regarding the relationship between the local and the global among forum participants. Reformists, traditional leftists, and even some network-based movements are supportive of global institutions, while others argue that global institutions are inherently undemocratic in that they are too far removed from the realities of the local communities they are supposed to serve. In this sense, for example, rather than building alternative global institutions, autonomous movements emphasize local self-management.

This issue of democracy and scale is perhaps most clearly revealed in the contrasting views of a hypothetical democratic world government among forum participants. According to the survey of participants at the 2005 WSF, the majority of respondents (68 percent) think that a democratic world government would be a good idea, although only 29 percent of these think this is actually plausible. By contrast, 32 percent of participants think that a democratic world government is a bad idea.[2] In this sense, whereas most participants surveyed at the 2005 WSF hold radical views regarding capitalism and current global institutions, fewer hold radical views regarding the state. This suggests that respondents were more likely to hold views associated with institutional actors and the traditional left than network-based or autonomous movements. Indeed, as discussed in Chapter 2,

Table 4.3   Responses to the question: Do you think it is a good or bad idea to have a democratic world government?

Response	Valid Percentage
Good idea, and it's plausible	29
Good idea, but not plausible	39
Bad idea	32
More than one answer	1

Source: University of California–Riverside survey (see Reese et al. 2006)

Note: Number of responses: 545.

network-based movements and their autonomous counterparts, in particular, are much less likely to participate in the social forums, and when they do, they are more likely to organize within various autonomous spaces during the forums.

Electoral Politics or Grassroots Organizing

A final and related ideological and political fault line among forum participants has to do with their view of the relationship between social movements and the state. In general, reformist actors and traditional leftists view the state as a legitimate terrain of struggle. In this sense, the forums not only serve to discuss and generate alternatives, they are also developing concrete proposals that can be adopted by political parties. Radicals, on the other hand, including some network-based and most autonomous movements, reject electoral politics, focusing instead on grassroots organizing and local self-management. This divide reflects the tension between networking and command logics within the forum process more generally (Juris 2008).

More specifically, there has been an ongoing debate regarding the role of political parties inside the forum process (Chapter 3). As we saw in Chapter 2, the WSF Charter forbids the participation of political parties, clearly stating, "Neither party representations nor military organizations shall participate in the Forum." At the same time, however, the next sentence goes on to point out that "government leaders and members of legislatures who accept the commitments of this Charter may be invited to participate in a personal capacity." In other words, the WSF is clearly defined as a civil society initiative, but there is significant ambiguity regarding the actual role of political parties within the process, as we saw in Chapter 3. Although many reformists and traditional leftists applaud this participation, network-based and autonomous movements are critical of it, arguing that political leaders are trying to take advantage of the forum for their own electoral purposes.

Reform-Oriented Proposals

This section outlines some of the specific proposals for political and economic reforms that have been discussed within and around the forum process. These are not only supported by institutional actors but also by many traditional leftists and network-based movements as a first step toward more radical change. However, as suggested above, many network-based and autonomous movements, including those who organize within autonomous spaces within and around the forums, reject concrete reforms entirely.

The Bamako Appeal and the G19 Declaration

The G19 declaration is a series of action proposals developed by a group of nineteen prominent intellectuals and released on January 29, 2005, during the 2005 WSF in Porto Alegre. The Bamako Appeal, produced by eighty prominent figures at the Bamako, Mali, Polycentric WSF in 2006, is similar but includes a longer discussion of proposals for building another world and is meant to consolidate the gains made at previous meetings (Karides and Frezzo 2006). With an emphasis on constructing a global south-north internationalism and building a cultural, political, and economic consensus, the Bamako Appeal is an invitation to act on the collective consciousness that is developing as a result of the forum process.

Although the G19 declaration (also referred to as the "Consensus of Porto Alegre") and Bamako Appeal were written collectively, they do not represent the WSF as a single body. Indeed, many WSF participants have criticized these documents for their perceived attempt to represent the voice of the entire forum, thus violating the WSF Charter of Principles. Although the Bamako Appeal is now more widely discussed among WSF participants, the G19 proposal provides a similar, but more succinct set of proposals. We review the G19 declaration to provide a snapshot of many of the important reform-oriented proposals being discussed within and around the forum process. The specific proposals, most of which enjoy widespread support among forum participants, include the following:

1. Cancel the public debt of southern countries, which has already been paid over many times and thus constitutes, for creditor states, financial establishments, and international financial institutions, the best way to keep the largest part of humanity under its control and keep it in misery.

2. Apply international taxes to financial transactions (especially the Tobin Tax with respect to speculative currency transactions), direct foreign investments, profits generated by transnational corporations, the sale of weapons, and activities that emit substantial amounts of greenhouse gases.

3. Progressively dismantle all forms of fiscal, juridical, and banking paradises, which are nothing more than refuges for organized crime, corruption, and all kinds of trafficking, fraud, and fiscal evasions, as well as criminal operations by large companies and even governments.

4. Each inhabitant of the planet should have the right to work, to receive social security, and to retire, respecting equality among men and women, making this an imperative of national and international public policy.

5. Promote all forms of fair trade, rejecting the free trade rules of the World Trade Organization and putting into practice mechanisms that allow for production processes in goods and services to move progressively toward the highest social norms (as indicated in the conventions of the International Labour Organization) and environmental norms. Completely exclude education, health, social services, and culture from the sphere of the WTO General Agreement on Trade in Services. The convention on cultural diversity, which is currently being negotiated by the United Nations Educational, Scientific, and Cultural Organization (UNESCO), should make the prevalence of cultural rights over trade rights explicit.

6. Guarantee the right to food sovereignty and security to each country and the promotion of peasant agriculture. This would mean the complete cancellation of subventions for exporting agricultural products, mainly by the United States and European Union, and the possibility of applying taxes to imports to prevent dumping practices.[3] In the same way, each country or group of countries should be able to decide under its own sovereignty to prohibit the production and importation of genetically modified organisms meant for food.

7. Prohibit all patents of knowledge and living things (human, animal, or vegetable), as well as all privatization of the common goods of humanity, particularly water.

The G19 declaration goes on to argue that "Another Possible World" should promote living together in peace and justice, at the scale of all humanity. Therefore, it is necessary to:

8. Fight, in the first place, for public policies against all discrimination, sexism, xenophobia, anti-Semitism, and

racism. Fully recognize the political, cultural, and economic rights (including the control over natural resources) of indigenous peoples.

9. Take urgent measures to put an end to the destruction of the environment and the threat of grave climate change due to the greenhouse effect, resulting mainly from the proliferation of individual vehicles and the excessive use of nonrenewable energies. Begin to put into place another development model based on efficient use of energy and the democratic control of natural resources, and drinking water in particular, around the world.

10. Demand the dismantling of foreign military bases and troops in all countries, except those which act under the expressed mandate of the United Nations.

And furthermore "Another Possible World" should promote democracy from local neighborhoods to the entire planet. Therefore, it is necessary to:

11. Guarantee the right of citizens to information and the right to inform through legislation that (a) ends the concentration of media in the hands of giant communication groups; (b) guarantees the autonomy of journalists with respect to investors; (c) favors the nonprofit press, in particular alternative and community media. The respect for these rights implies citizen counterpower, particularly in the form of national and international observatories of communications media.

12. Reform and profoundly democratize international organizations, among them the UN, emphasizing human, economic, social, and cultural rights, in accord with the Universal Declaration on Human Rights. This means the incorporation of the World Bank, the Inter-

national Monetary Fund, and the WTO into the system and decisionmaking mechanisms of the UN. If the United States continues to violate international law, move the headquarters of the UN out of New York and toward another country, preferably in the south.

Mural of Proposals

In contrast to the G19 declaration (and the Bamako Appeal), the Mural of Proposals was first launched in 2005 as a completely open process to which anyone could contribute, and thus better reflects the forum's open space methodology and ideals. At the same time, however, although the Mural of Proposals embodies the horizontal, collaborative process promoted by the forum, the lists are extremely long, and concrete proposals can be easily lost in the shuffle. During its first year, the Mural of Proposals archived 306 proposals collected within the forum's 12 thematic "World Social Territories." Although many of the proposals are oriented toward specific reforms, most involve calls for various forms of action among participants in local, continental, and global contexts.[4] Some of the specific reform-oriented proposals archived as part of the 2005 Mural of Proposals include:

- Exclusion of water from the process of privatization through the reinforcement of public water systems (continental level)
- Creation of transgenic-free areas by supporting the initiative of the Brazilian state of Parana to create a zone free of genetically modified organisms (local level)
- Action against the Brazilian National Telecommunications Agency to ensure free access to information (national level)

- Interregional action network to facilitate coordinated actions against human trafficking involving NGOs and in cooperation with the UN and WSF (global level)
- A UNESCO convention on cultural diversity that would restrict culture from WTO-led liberalization agreements (global level)
- Millennium Development Goals campaign to raise public awareness and lobby world leaders to take action to reach the goals by 2015, as stipulated in the 2000 agreement (global level)
- Brazilian Action to Combat Inequality: a civil society campaign to combat inequality in Brazil (national level)
- New rules for a new economy: a new global governance regime to move from grassroots experiences to a fair global economy (global level)
- Campaign for the Democratic Construction of a Social Responsibility Law in Brazil (national level)
- Global Currency Transaction Tax Campaign (CTTC) to pressure governments around the world to implement a CTTC (global level)
- Regional governance and a South American Community of Nations to promote the participation of civil society in a South American Community of Nations (continental level)
- Organization of United Peoples to create a global civil society institution independent of the United Nations (global level)
- Global campaign to reduce military defense spending and promote nonviolent systems of defense and civil intervention (global level)
- Fair trade for all Latin Americans: create laws that help artisan and small producer organizations open and develop fair and sustainable trade stores (continental level)

- Creation of a world parliament elected by the people (based on one person, one vote) that is the most important institution for the creation of international law (global level)

Radical Visions

Many of the radical ideas, visions, and practices within the social forums can be found along the margins, particularly in the youth camps and various autonomous spaces surrounding the official forum. For its part, the International Youth Camp (IYC) began as an emergency solution to the problem of housing during the first WSF in Porto Alegre (Nunes 2005). The camp was led by traditional Brazilian youth organizations, including leftist parties and formal student movements. As such, the camp exhibited little evidence of a new horizontal form of organization, and the camp was located in a large urban park far from the center of activities. Moreover, the camp featured little programming. All this began to change with the second IYC and the increasing participation of newer political actors from gay rights, homelessness, and hip hop movements. In particular, the participation of autonomous architecture students led to the concept of the youth camp as a city, involving self-managed, directly democratic forms of organization, and an increased presence of alternative media and ecologically friendly construction techniques (Nunes 2005; Juris 2005a).

The concept of the youth camp as a city was taken even further during the 2005 edition of the IYC in Porto Alegre. The idea was to transform the camp from an alternative sleeping area into an innovative space for generating new forms of social, political, and cultural interaction. Specifically, the IYC was organized into zones around seven Action Centers intended to promote the convergence of activities around similar themes.

These included the Caracol Intergaláctika (global struggles, new forms of activism, and direct action), Espaço Che (culture and health), Laboratório de Conhecimentos Livres (free knowledge and communication), Lôgun Édé (human rights and sexual diversity), Terrau (anticapitalist social movements), Raizes (cultures of resistance), and Tupiguara (environmental culture). There were also numerous *axônios,* or smaller spaces, scattered throughout the camp, housing activities related to feminism, health, clowning, hip-hop, solidarity economies, student movements, and religion. Cultural forms of intervention were also prevalent throughout the camp. Moreover, the Caracol Intergaláctika involved debates surrounding direct action, autonomous politics and horizontality, intellectual property rights, activist research, and critiques of the official forum.

Significantly, the 2005 IYC was organized along self-managed, directly democratic lines. As pointed out above, radical network-based and autonomous movements emphasize horizontal coordination and local self-management, thus expressing their political visions as much through concrete action as discourse. In this sense, residents were encouraged to take part in construction, administration, and decisionmaking tasks. Indeed, the camp was conceived as a laboratory for generating network-based social and political practices. As their organizing manual pointed out, the IYC was designed to "create a short-circuit in the old forms of political representation. It's a laboratory of the new political militancy seeking to make resistance an act of creation, to promote counter-power." Whereas many of the workshops in the official forum emphasized critiques of the current global political and economic system and offered reform-oriented solutions, the IYC represented a model of what an alternative world might look like beyond the market and state, involving local self-management and new models of horizontal organization. Participants in the IYC and the forum at large raise the point that while IYC begins to enact another world, the older generation stays in hotels and meets in bars, reinforcing generational gaps (Guay 2005).

The 2005 IYC also offered programming around several thematic areas that form part of an emerging radical vision among global justice activists. These include autonomy, squatting, the commons, alternative economies, renewable energy, independent media, free software, and "copyleft" (as opposed to traditional copyrights). Many of these have also been addressed within official forums, as well as various autonomous spaces.

Autonomy

One of the primary goals among radical anticorporate globalization activists from both network-based and autonomous movements is the achievement of social, political, cultural, and economic autonomy. In this sense, rather than struggling for political reforms, grassroots radicals are more interested in developing local forms of self-management in diverse areas of social life. The 2005 IYC thus offered numerous workshops related to the vision and practice of autonomy. For example, several discussions in the Caracol Intergaláctika involved the sharing of ideas and experiences regarding grassroots struggles for autonomous self-management, including worker-run factories in Argentina, autonomous Zapatista communities, autonomous media projects, and self-managed social centers. Moreover, the goal of autonomy runs through each of the thematic areas discussed below.

Squatting

One way radical grassroots activists are struggling for autonomy is through the practice of squatting, which involves taking over abandoned buildings or unused land and transforming those places into self-managed communities. The 2005 IYC housed several discussions and workshops around squatting, with a particular focus on the Brazilian Landless Workers Movement (MST) and squatted social centers around Europe, North, and South America. The MST is a particularly interesting example, involving a mass social movement where landless workers squat unused, privately owned farmland and create their own self-run communities. Squatted social centers, on the other hand, largely involve an urban youth-based movement, where young people take over abandoned buildings in order to have access to cheap housing and build autonomous spaces for alternative forms of social, cultural, and political interaction. Squatting thus represents a concrete way of developing local autonomy from and within capitalist social and economic relations. Opportunities to engage in this practice depend on local political, economic, and demographic conditions. Squats are easier to conduct within less repressive regimes and in areas that are becoming less populous or where factories and land are unused.

The Commons

Another important concept emerging within more radical anti-corporate globalization circles within and around the forums involves the commons. Rather than simply opposing the privatization of land, water, energy, and other natural resources, a focus on the commons suggests the importance of collectively controlling and self-managing communal resources. In this sense, local autonomy and self-management are emphasized over state-based solutions, such as nationalization. The commons thus implies an emerging noncapitalist vision for autonomously managing vital resources, which is inspired by both older forms of communal organization and new forms of decentralized organization and horizontal coordination. Several workshops addressed this theme during the 2005 IYC, such as the Caracol Intergaláctika as well as the Terrau (anticapitalist social movements) and Tupiguara (environmental culture) zones. Moreover, an entire alternative conference—Life Despite Capitalism—was dedicated to the commons as part of the autonomous spaces during the 2004 European Social Forum in London.

Alternative Economies

Another important goal among more radical grassroots actors involves the creation of an alternative economy that exists outside global capitalism. Among the many projects discussed in and around the forums, particularly in the various youth camps and autonomous spaces, this economy involves the creation of alternative networks of collective production and distribution, free shops where people can exchange goods and services without monetary transactions, and the development of alternative currencies to facilitate economic transactions beyond capitalism.

In 2005, alternative currency projects were discussed within both the IYC and the official forum. In fact, an entire World Social Territory—"Sovereign Economies by and for the People"—was dedicated to this theme. Specific alternative currency projects discussed within and around the 2005 WSF included the creation of a global social currency; building "sovereign" economies based on traditional indigenous practices; the use of complementary currency systems (CCS) as a form of local monetary reorganization and resistance to global capitalism; and the exchange of experiences among specific alternative money initiatives, including the European Project Sol, Argentine barter club networks, and the Local Economic Transfer System (LETS), a directly democratic community enterprise that uses a scoring system to facilitate nonmonetary exchange. As we see in Chapter 5, discussions of alternative or solidarity economy projects transcend some of the radical/reformist distinctions emphasized here and are found in a variety of forum settings.

Renewable Energy

Another important aspect of the more radical visions being discussed within and around the social forums involves the need to develop renewable energy sources as the basis for building a truly sustainable alternative to the current global capitalist system, including hydropower-, wind-, solar-, geothermal-, and biomass-derived energy. Numerous renewable energy workshops were organized during the 2005 IYC, particularly in the Tupiguara (environmental culture) zone, as well as the World Social Territory in the official forum dedicated to "Assuring and Defending the Earth and People's Common Goods." Moreover, as pointed out above, the entire youth camp was constructed using recycled materials and ecologically sustainable methods, suggesting the importance of concrete practice within more radical circles.

Independent Media

The development of alternative media has been one of the most important features of global justice movements (Juris 2005b). More radical network-based movements in particular have pioneered the use of new digital technologies for autonomously creating and distributing self-managed media content produced by and for grassroots social movements. In particular, since the Independent Media Center (IMC), or Indymedia, was founded in Seattle during the November 1999 protests against the WTO, a global network of Indymedia Centers has emerged, involving more than 160 local sites around the world. Temporary IMCs have also been set up during global protests and gatherings, including local, world, and regional social forums.

During the 2005 edition of the WSF, for example, the IYC housed an Independent Media Center as well as an entire zone for creating and sharing autonomously produced audio, video, and software called the "Laboratory of Free Knowledge." Meanwhile, the official forum also dedicated a World Social Territory to "Communication: Counter-Hegemonic Practices, Rights and Alternatives." Other independent media projects within and around the 2005 WSF included the International Independent Information Exchange, which provided a web-based forum for posting and distributing news stories related to the WSF (www.ciranda.net); a Radio Forum, involving community stations from around the world and webcast 24 hours a day; as well as a TV Forum, which coordinated video recordings and created a one-hour television show. For radical activists, independent media are not only critical tools facilitating social movement organizing; they also prefigure an alternative, noncapitalist world in which news and information are autonomously controlled by the communities and groups that use them.

Free Software and Copyleft

Finally, another important component of creating truly autonomous media systems is the creation and distribution of free software (FS). Since the 2004 edition of the WSF in Mumbai, organizers have made a concerted effort to use free software, including GNU/Linux operating systems, on all forum-related computer networks (Caruso 2005).[5] Free software is nonproprietary and based on open source development principles, where computer programmers improve and distribute new versions of software code through collaborative networks (Juris 2008). Free software thus requires the right to distribute and access source code, posing a challenge to corporate software monopolies, such as Microsoft. The 2005 WSF in Porto Alegre ran free software on all 1,000 computers and shifted the official website to an open source language, while the 2005 IYC also ran free software on all computer systems (Milan 2005).

Free software is a specific example of a more general legal principle and license called copyleft, which explicitly states that any person can use, modify, and redistribute written documents and computer software, as well as works of art and music. For radicals, free software and copyleft pose a major challenge to the intellectual property rights regime on which the current global capitalist order depends, establishing the basis for an alternative political and economic system. Numerous workshops were organized around free software and copyleft during the 2005 IYC, particularly in the Laboratory of Free Knowledge Zone, as well as the official forum within a World Social Territory dedicated to "Autonomous Thought, Reappropriation and Social-ization of Knowledge and Technologies."

Conclusion

This chapter has explored the main social movement sectors that have participated in the social forum process, including their alternative visions and goals. As we have seen, institutional actors are more likely to support concrete reforms, while traditional leftists and network-based and autonomous movements are more interested in radical initiatives. At the same time, however, traditional leftists and network-based movements often support reforms as a step toward long-term structural change, and many of the more radical proposals discussed here are finding a broader base of support among the diverse groups coming together in the WSF process. This is not surprising, as the ide-ologies articulated by global justice activists resist the traditional dualisms offered in conventional discourses and institutions.

We have also examined some of the specific political and ideological tensions within and around the forums, with a par-ticular focus on debates such as reform or revolution, democra-tize vs. abolish global institutions, world government vs. local organizing, and electoral politics vs. grassroots self-management. Survey data suggest that most WSF participants want to abolish and replace capitalism, although nearly 40 percent seek to reform it. These data also suggest that participants are more likely to hold such radical anticapitalist perspectives if they belong to self-funded political organizations, parties, and movements. An even greater portion (about 84 percent of those answering the question and 80 percent of all survey respondents) also favor the abolition of the IMF and WTO, with most respondents favoring their replacement with more democratic alternatives. The most radical ideas around autonomy and self-management are more likely to be found within the youth camps and autonomous spaces along the margins of the forum. Finally, we also outlined some of the myriad proposals for both concrete reforms and more radical, antisystemic initiatives within and around the forum process. Indeed, the WSF can be seen as a laboratory for generating innovative ideas and alternatives.

Chapter Five
GLOBAL OR LOCAL: WHERE'S THE ACTION?

I n Chapter 1, we characterized the WSF process as one that emerged creatively in a world of growing economic hardship for most and in the context of the closing of democratic spaces. Participants in the WSF process have come together to challenge their exclusion from what have become increasingly globalized decisionmaking processes within the global polity and capitalist economy that affect policies and experiences at local and national levels. WSF participants also challenge the international diffusion of various repressive, restrictive, and intolerant ideas and practices that are associated with neoliberalism, such as neo-conservatism, racism, nativism, and Christian or Islamic funda-mentalism. They also challenge the foreign policies of the United States and other powerful nations. During its first several years of existence the WSF has evolved, and it continues to transform itself in response to several creative tensions that are inherent to global democracy. As previous chapters showed, the tensions between vertical and horizontal groups, the challenges of expanding participation by marginalized groups, the best ways to work with more powerful political actors, along with questions of how to remain an open space for deliberation while also facilitating action, are important issues in the WSF process. Here we will explore the conflicts between local and global scales of political action.

Shortly after the first WSF in 2001, activists working at local and regional levels began organizing parallel forums that made explicit connections to the WSF process.[1] This demonstrates the possibilities of the "political imagination" that has been inspired by the WSF's declaration that "another world is possible." It also shows that this process builds on a longer history of transnational political action through which activists have learned and communicated new ways of engaging in politics beyond their national borders. We see this proliferation of social forums in different locations as a form of *political improvisation* that mirrors jazz performances: players demonstrate the uniqueness of their instruments and their own creativity while maintaining rhythmic and tonal connections with the group (Wainwright 2004). In the global picture, the WSF might be seen as an ensemble of assemblies of individuals linked by their commitment to key principles that bounce across diverse locales and scales of action. As social forums are manifested in a given place, they take on unique sounds, bringing in fresh complexities and textures along with the new voices and issues that enter the mix. Just as when the saxophone player yields to the bass solo, when social forums move from one region or locale to another, we notice new elements of the tune. We may hear more or less dissonance in the musicians' interpretation of a melody, and yet when the soloist rejoins the whole ensemble, we remember the underlying unity and coherence of the song. The networking among activists and the shared understandings that arise from transborder communications and a history of transnational campaigning allow action taking place at multiple sites and scales to contribute to a more or less harmonious global performance.

Geographic Proliferation of Social Forums

The WSF as a single *world* forum changed its format in 2006 when the WSF International Council (IC) responded to the tensions activists expressed between global and more localized scales of organizing by experimenting with a polycentric social forum. That year, the WSF met in sequence in three cities: Bamako, Mali; Caracas, Venezuela; and Karachi, Pakistan. The International Council decided to suspend the centralized world gathering in 2008 to make room for more geographically proximate and thematic forums.

The tension driving this evolution in the form of the WSF is that expressed by organizers working simultaneously to nurture transnational and world-level dialogues about contemporary struggles while also expanding local and national organizing efforts. Discussions among organizers demonstrate the very real challenges of building democracy on a global scale: one has to simultaneously cultivate wide, global networks and understandings while also doing the hard work of empowering local communities and bridging local, national, and transnational social change efforts. This work involves helping local communities understand how local problems are linked to, and can be challenged through, global institutions and structures. It also involves helping transnational activists to learn from local and national activists how global processes are experienced and understood locally and how best to support organizing that is already under way at local, national, or regional scales.

The experience in the international and regional organizing committees suggested a continuing need for global and regional forums to help local communities relate their demands to broader debates and analyses, and to cultivate shared understandings and identities among diverse communities. Yet the work it takes to arrange the logistics of bringing thousands of people to regional or world meetings took a toll on organizers whose local activism was sidelined as they worked to build organizing committees and make the arrangements necessary for such forums to take place. The very practice of organizing large-scale events encompasses the tension between local and global levels of activism.

Regional social forums—starting with the first European Social Forum, in Florence, in 2002; followed by the first Asian Social Forum, in Hyderabad, in 2003; the first Social Forum of the Americas, in Quito, and the first African Social Forum, in Conakry, both in 2004; as well as thematic social forums, like the first Pan-Amazon Social Forum, held in Belém, in 2002—have all been convened on a yearly basis in most cases, and they have drawn tens of thousands of participants, with the European meetings drawing the largest crowds.[2] Regional social forums have reflected both the degree of integration as well as cleavage and conflict in their respective macroregions, just as national social forums have done. Thematic forums have been convened to address priority issues. These have included a forum on the Argentine financial crisis in 2002; another on democracy, human rights, war, and drug trafficking in Colombia; a Border Social Forum in Ciudad Juárez/El Paso focusing on immigrants' rights; and a Canadian forum focusing on peace. Activists have also organized hundreds of national and local forums not formally tied—but nonetheless linked—to the WSF process. Table 5.1 lists the main regional social forums, and Map 5.1 shows the locations of many local social forums, which are organized autonomously by local communities[3] and therefore harder to track systematically. Map 5.1 likely illustrates an undercount of the true number of local social forums, and its authors noted that they did not provide full records for the countries of Italy and Greece because of the sheer volume of local social forum activity (Glasius and Timms 2006).

Table 5.1   Regional Social Forums

Regional Forum	Location, Date
European Social Forum	Florence, November 2002 Paris, November 2003 London, October 2004 Athens, May 2006
Social Forum of the Americas	Quito, Ecuador, July 2004 Caracas, Venezuela, January 2006
Mediterranean Social Forum	Barcelona, June 2005
Caribbean Social Forum	Martinique, July 2006
Asian Social Forum	Hyderabad, India, January 2003
African Social Forum	Addis Ababa, Ethiopia, 2003
Pan-Amazonian Social Forum	Belém, Brazil, January 2002, 2003 Ciudad Guayana, Venezuela, February 2004 Manaus, Amazonas, January 2005

Source: www.forumsocialmundial.org.br/quadro_frc.php?cd_forum=9.

We see from Table 5.1 and Map 5.1 that Europe and South America have been most active in the WSF process, but that every world region has seen some regional and local social forum activity. The organization of more localized forums in Asia and Africa was part of the effort to organize the centralized world forum in those regions. These preliminary meetings reflect the reciprocal effects of the global level on more geographically proximate organizing efforts.

One puzzle confronting those who seek to understand the WSF process is the relative absence of U.S. citizens in this global process.[4] Despite the fact that the protest against the World Trade Organization in Seattle was one of the precursors to the WSF, U.S. activists have not participated in large numbers at most WSFs, and local- and regional-level organizing in North

Map 5.1 Local Social Forums by Type

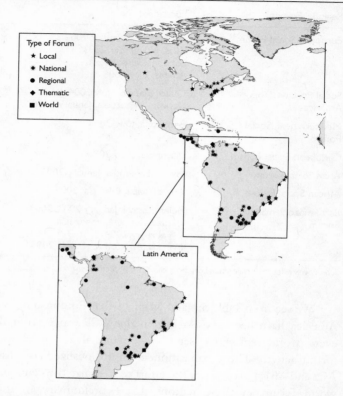

Source: Glasius, Marlies, and Jill Timms. 2006. "The Role of Social Forums in Global Civil Society: Radical Beacon or Strategic Infrastructure," in *Global Civil Society Yearbook,* 2005/6, edited by M. Glasius, M. Kaldor, and H. Anheier. Thousand Oaks, Calif.: Sage, pp. 196–197.

America has been limited. Table 5.2 records the local and regional forums in the United States that we have been able to document.[5]

The relative absence of U.S. activists is all the more baffling since U.S. organizers have played important leadership roles in transnational human rights and other initiatives. For example, Jody

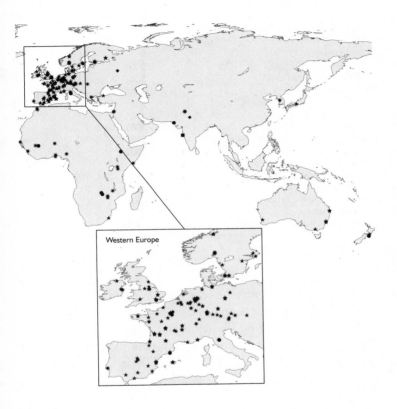

Western Europe

Williams earned the Nobel Peace Prize for her work on the International Campaign to Ban Landmines, and U.S. activists were key players in the campaign for an International Criminal Court.[6]

But there is also a long tradition in U.S. politics of "American exceptionalism" that views the United States as above the fray of the international system, autonomous of the need to negotiate with other nations to solve shared problems or manage resources. The U.S. public, moreover, remains largely misinformed about the

**Table 5.2   Local, Regional, and National Social Forums in
the United States**

	Years
Local Forums	
Boston Social Forum	2004
Chicago Social Forum	2005; 2006
Houston Social Forum	2006
Los Angeles Social Forum	2007
Maine Social Forum	2006
New York Social Forum	2002; 2003
Puerto Rico Social Forum	2006
San Francisco Social Forum	2002
Regional Forums	
Midwest Social Forum	2004; 2005; 2006
Southeast Social Forum	2006
Border Social Forum	2006
National Forum	
United States Social Forum	2007

world and their country's role within it. Many people in the
United States see their country as generous in its aid policies and
benevolent in its support for democracy and peace in the world,
and the mainstream media reinforces this misleading picture (see,
e.g., Kull et al. 2003). But for many involved in the WSF process,
U.S. foreign policy is a major obstacle to making another world
possible. Thus, U.S. activists hoping to expand public awareness
and attention to global issues face important hurdles as they seek
to draw U.S. citizens' attention to the ways civil society actors
have been working cooperatively to confront challenges of economic inequality, environmental degradation, and especially the
erosion of democracy around the world.

One thing we see in Table 5.2, however, is that—in terms of
local and national organizing—U.S. activists may be coming late
to the WSF party rather than ignoring it altogether. Most of the
U.S. local and regional forums have happened in very recent

years, and some can be directly linked to the preparations for the U.S. Social Forum in 2007. For instance, during 2005 there were regional forums in the southeastern and midwestern parts of the United States and on the southwest border as well as a Puerto Rico social forum. Each of these forums drew hundreds of activists. The attacks on the World Trade Center and Pentagon in the United States in 2001 certainly transformed the U.S. political agenda in ways that complicated efforts to organize around global economic justice (although U.S. activist participation in the first WSF in January 2001 was already very low). Also, since September 2001, many U.S. activists have been preoccupied with efforts to defend basic democratic rights and to oppose U.S. military intervention overseas, diverting much attention from other global justice campaigns. This may have delayed U.S. citizens' responses to the WSF. But the evidence here suggests that the pendulum is swinging back toward more outward-looking responses to the challenges our world now faces, and we may see more engagement in the WSF process by citizens of the world's largest military and economic power. Such participation is crucial for this global effort to make another world possible.

Social Forums and Spaces of Action

While we've focused thus far on the proliferation of social forums from a centralized world meeting to regional and local settings, these meetings actually represent just the tip of the iceberg of the actual political organizing work being done by WSF participants. Although activists actually gather for just a few days, they work together for many months prior to the event, and many also follow up their participation in the WSF process by launching new campaigns, developing new organizational strategies, or joining new coalitions. The real action of the social forums is not in the meeting spaces themselves—although these gatherings are clearly very important. Rather, the WSF process ripples into the ongoing activities of the individuals and organizers that are part of the process. To return to our jazz ensemble metaphor, the performance itself represents just a fraction of the effort and capabilities of participating musicians, and time spent practicing and preparing for a given performance can itself generate new relationships while inspiring new ideas and initiatives. This continued activism ensures that future social forums are new iterations revisiting the concerns established in earlier meetings but moving the agenda of the social forum forward.

The work to organize the logistics of the forums themselves brings groups together across organizational and issue divisions that organizers might otherwise never cross. The process of planning plenary sessions and workshops for the forums ideally involves discussions over time about how best to organize within the social forum setting. As people gain more experience with the forums, they have learned to make better use of the networking possibilities therein. Indeed, more people are beginning to use the process to launch new and more effective conversations and brainstorming sessions about how to improve popular mobilizing for a more just and peaceful world. Over time, and through multiple interactions across cultural, class, and national divides, people learn new ways of thinking and acting in response to global challenges.

Since the WSF challenges global capitalism and its democratic deficits, much discussion at forum events centers on ideas about alternative ways of organizing economic life. Although the forums themselves may be experiments in how to create spaces for democratic deliberation about policy, they are also venues where concrete ideas for restructuring economic power can be discussed, refined, and spread. Those protesting against the predominant form of economic globalization are creating new spaces in which locally empowering economic practices can flourish. It is through such local practices that many WSF participants hope to make the ideals of the WSF a reality.

At the first WSF the Global Network of the Solidarity Socioeconomy was established. This network of solidarity economies has grown to include forty-seven national and regional solidarity economy networks and includes tens of thousands of democratic grassroots economic initiatives worldwide. Solidarity economy was heavily emphasized in the content of the polycentric WSF in Venezuela in 2006. Solidarity economy approaches, emerging in Latin America in the mid-1980s and expanding throughout the 1990s, discredit the singular view of the profit-oriented market exchange of neoliberalism—emphasizing instead a plural view of economy "in which individuals, communities, and organizations generate livelihoods through many different means and with many different motivations and aspirations" (Miller 2006). The solidarity economy idea begins from the recognition that, although human societies largely depend on cooperation and mutual support, economic life under capitalism is organized to encourage only competitive relationships. It holds that our economies must be reorganized to reinforce the cooperative social networks necessary to support human communities. In the following, we highlight examples of these initiatives, which have been discussed at typical social forum gatherings.[7]

Community-Supported Agriculture (CSA)

Modern agriculture has made farming increasingly reliant on fossil-fuel, more mechanized, more large-scale, and less profitable for farmers. Much of the money spent on food today goes not to the farmer, but to retailers, shippers, manufacturers, and marketing firms. And as food markets go global, those producing our food have less control over how and what they can produce. Corporate agriculture has reduced the ability of local communities to feed themselves and increased dependence on transnational corporations. It is not surprising, then, that many farmers participate in the WSFs as well as regional and local forums. Participants at WSFs are increasingly organizing around the demand for food sovereignty as a means of local empowerment. Via Campesina, for instance, a large global network of farmers from around the world has been a major proponent of food sovereignty and a member of the International Council of the WSF. Its members are very active in the WSF process and have actively promoted food sovereignty initiatives such as community-supported agriculture (CSAs) organizations.

CSAs are a form of solidarity economics through which farmers transform economic relations at the base of the food chain. Essentially, they reorganize the food economy to shorten the distance between producer and consumer. CSA members pay farmers an annual membership fee to cover the production costs of the farm, and in return they receive a weekly share of the harvest during the local growing season. CSAs help spread the risks and costs of farming by providing farmers with financing at the beginning of the season, thereby reducing or eliminating the need for costly loans, while ensuring a predictable income for their harvest. By creating direct relationships between local farmers and community members, CSAs enable small-scale producers to thrive while enhancing local food security and sovereignty. CSAs also help raise consumers' awareness of how their food choices impact both the economic realities of the wider community as well as the environment.

Community Currencies and Barter Systems

Community currency and barter systems build on the notion that money is a creation of our political institutions and that it needs to be distinguished from real wealth. National and international monetary systems, they argue, make communities vulnerable to external economic forces over which they have no influence. They also devalue goods and services that local communities see as important. For instance, unemployed or under-employed workers may not be able to gain dollars or pesos or yen for their work, but these people's skills can still be useful to the local community. At the local level, there are children to care for, parks and public spaces to maintain, senior citizens needing assistance, and local gardens to tend. What is lacking is a means for communities to reward work that is necessary and beneficial for the community itself. Fresh produce or locally produced artwork may not have markets outside a local area, but residents of an area may be willing to pay more for such goods, given that they taste better and that they were produced by people in the community.

Local currencies allow communities themselves to determine what goods and services they value. Often these initiatives grow from communities where a large corporate employer suddenly moves out of the town, causing widespread unemployment and encouraging job-seekers to leave their communities in search of work. Or they emerge in places where rapid inflation undermines people's economic security, as happened in the late 1990s and early 2000s in parts of Asia and Latin America. The "Ithaca Hours" currency in Ithaca, New York, has been operating since the early 1990s, and it has inspired many other communities to print their own money in order to gain more control over local economic choices. Workshops at WSFs have allowed people to exchange experiences on organizing local currency and barter initiatives that can help protect them from the external shocks of the global economy. For instance, activists from Argentina developed these types of projects in response to the collapse of their economy in 2001, and they shared their insights and experiences with their international counterparts in the social forums. Regional and local forums also allow for the transfer of ideas and organizing insights, and at the Midwest Social Forum in Milwaukee in 2006, organizers of a Humboldt

County (California) local currency project discussed their work with interested activists from around the United States.[8]

Cooperative Ownership

Social movements have helped advance cooperative ownership models for economic production by organizing such initiatives and encouraging the public to support cooperative production. Many local examples of such cooperatives exist in virtually every part of the world. Perhaps the most important large-scale example of this kind of initiative is in Argentina, where workers arranged to take ownership of enterprises that failed in the wake of that country's economic collapse. They collectively assumed the risks of ownership of the production facilities, and most of the surviving cooperatives have generated wages for workers that are equal to or more than wages before the economic crisis. The WSF has supported economic cooperatives by purchasing goods and services needed for these huge gatherings from them. The WSFs also make it a point to inform WSF participants about how forum materials were produced, enhancing awareness of alternative economic models, and possibly inspiring new efforts to support and promote them.

Fair Trade Programs

The global economy is organized around the assumption that if governments create policies that encourage the investment of capital to produce profits, the whole of society will benefit (eventually, at least) as wealth "trickles down." Thus, tax policies, government subsidies and spending programs, and investments in infrastructures (such as roadways and energy systems) are organized with the aim of helping promote economic growth and profits for wealthy investors and major corporations. Many have argued that these policies don't work and that social programs and policies need to promote more than profit-seeking and economic growth. They must also aim to promote other social goals, such as quality education and health care, environmental sustainability, preservation of leisure time, opportunities for local ownership, protection of workers, equitable access to essential resources such as clean water, and wages that support a decent living for workers and families. These values are not factored into the prices of most goods. Fair trade programs are arrangements between consumers and producers that promote these other social values in more limited markets. By purchasing fair trade coffee and other goods, consumers contribute to economic empowerment of local producers and their communities, strengthening the possibilities for grassroots, bottom-up alternatives to a global economy to thrive. The WSF process is a global space where links can be made between producers and consumers who may wish to establish new fair trade arrangements or to improve existing ones. It also promotes greater awareness of the possibilities for more equitable trade relationships among participants.

Rethinking Corporate Structures

Another way social movements shape the prospects for economic democracy, or greater control by citizens over decisions affecting how they spend their time and money, is by working to bring greater scrutiny to transnational corporations that have become less subject to regulation by democratic (or any) governments. An important example of activism taking place within the WSF in this regard is the global antisweatshop campaign. Although this campaign emerged long before the WSF process and helped shape the broader global justice movement, many groups promoting better and more consistent application of labor protections have been a key part of the WSF process. Among the groups helping focus attention on this particular campaign are international labor unions, whose transnational structures have helped sensitize them to the consequences of neoliberalism in local settings (Bandy 2000; Munck 2002; Waterman 2005; Waterman and Timms 2004). At a time when governments are scaling back their regulatory policies to encourage international investment and trade, WSF activists are working directly to call on corporations to abandon the antisocial behaviors that free markets encourage. In the process, they are helping to define the criteria and mechanisms for corporate governance at a time when governments have adopted—voluntarily or not—a hands-off approach.

But while antisweatshop and labor-rights actions are important, these efforts are limited in their abilities to improve actual conditions of workers in poor countries. Addressing the systemic problems caused by economic globalization's intensified pressures on workers requires efforts to make governments more proactive and aggressive in defending social goods and in regulating the practices of corporations. Some WSF activists have therefore advocated new rules for the governance of corporations. One example of this is the campaign for legally binding "UN Norms for Business." The initiative is being advanced by a coalition of groups, including Rights and Accountability in Development (RAID); Amnesty International; and the International Network for Economic, Social, and Cultural Rights, together with other corporate accountability groups and coalitions (International Network for Economic, Social, and Cultural Rights 2005; Amnesty International 2004). This coalition has used the WSF and regional forums to promote information about these campaigns and to encourage groups to help make these norms legally binding through local actions.[9]

Also discussed in various social forums are efforts to restructure the corporate charters that governments issue to allow corporations to operate legally. These charters have evolved over time to make corporations legally equivalent to individual citizens and to restrict the legal liability of owners for damages their corporate entities cause. Groups such as the Program on Corporations, Law, and Democracy have worked to educate activists at the Boston Social Forum and elsewhere about possibilities to engage in local initiatives to expand public deliberations about corporate rights and to subject corporate rights and privileges to greater public scrutiny and governmental control. An example of one such campaign is the use of local referenda to regulate corporations' social and environmental practices.[10]

The key point we emphasize here is that the WSF process is manifested in the convergence of activists in set places for rather short times, but that the process itself represents a collection of political and economic activities that have much broader and deeper significance. Understanding the impacts of the process requires that we consider the wider effects of the formation of new relationships at forum events. It also requires that we see how the new ideas are dispersed within a context that supports and celebrates the unity in core values among the diverse array of forum participants. Next, we look at how participants in global and regional social forums view the relationships among local, national, and global political arenas.

Participant Views on Global-Local Politics

Results from the University of California–Riverside survey of WSF participants in 2005 indicate that there is strong support for *global* strategies for social change among most WSF participants (Reese et al. 2006). These survey results also suggest that the strength of this support depends on the type of global strategy and respondents' residence in a northern, or "core," country or a "peripheral," southern one. Tables 5.3 and 5.4 compare responses of all survey respondents: those from richer and more

Table 5.3   What Should Be Done about International Finance and Trade Institutions?

	All Respondents (%)	Global North (%)	Global South (%)
Negotiate with them	14	14	14
Abolish and replace them	61	71	57
Abolish them	25	15	28

Source: University of California–Riverside survey (see Reese et al. 2006).

Notes: Chi-square statistic comparing these categories (10.676) is significant at the .01 level (4 degrees of freedom). N = 577. Percentages may not equal 100 due to rounding.

industrialized nations (the global north) and those from poorer and less industrialized nations (the global south).[11]

As Table 5.3 shows, most survey respondents and most respondents from both the north and south indicated that they believed that existing international finance and trade institutions, such as the IMF and WTO, should be abolished and replaced with better international institutions. However, there is significantly greater support for replacing these institutions among respondents from the global north. Compared with respondents from the global north, a greater share of respondents from southern countries said that these institutions should simply be abolished (and not replaced). This is particularly true among respondents from the semiperiphery, or middle-income southern countries.

As we saw in Chapter 4, when asked if they thought a democratic world government was a good idea, most survey respondents (68 percent) agreed. However, just 29 percent of respondents thought that such a proposal was really plausible. Northern respondents were significantly more favorable and optimistic about this proposal than southern respondents. Whereas 84 percent of northern respondents claimed it was a good idea, only 68 percent of southern respondents did. This difference may reflect the experiences of democracy in the global south, where governments tend to be less responsive and open to effective citizen participation, and the global north, where there are relatively greater opportunities for democratic expression. About 38 percent of northern respondents also expressed the belief that this would be plausible, compared with only 26 percent of southern respondents.

Further analysis revealed that although there is strong support for creating democratic global governance institutions among WSF participants, most activists prioritized local strategies for social change over global ones. Sixty percent of all survey respondents indicated that the best approach to solving the problems created by global capitalism was to strengthen local communities, rather than strengthening nation-states or creating democratic global institutions. Given the considerable capacity and strength of northern states, it is not surprising that only 4 percent of northern respondents saw strengthening nation-states as an important strategy. Support for this strategy was higher among southern respondents (11 percent). Support was even higher among respondents from the periphery, or low-income southern countries. This is not surprising given that southern respondents' nation-states are often pressed to adopt structural adjustment policies and other unpopular measures by more

Table 5.4   Preferred Approaches to Solving Problems Created by Global Capitalism

	All Respondents (%)	Global North (%)	Global South (%)
Empower local communities	60	57	61
Strengthen nation-states	10	4	11
Create democratic global institutions	30	38	28

Source: University of California–Riverside survey (see Reese et al. 2006).

Notes: Chi-square statistic comparing global with local and national categories of responses (7.169) is significant at the .05 level (2 degrees of freedom). N = 506. Percentages may not equal 100 due to rounding.

powerful nation–states and global institutions. Almost one-third of respondents said that the strategy of creating democratic global institutions was the most important for resolving global social problems. Support for this response is significantly weaker among southern than among northern respondents.[12]

In sum, these survey results suggest that among WSF participants, there is broad support for proposals to democratize global governance institutions and to empower local communities. However, participants from the global north and south differed in how much trust they have that democratically accountable global institutions are in fact possible and how much to prioritize local versus national or global initiatives. Although only 11 percent of southern respondents said that strengthening the nation-state was the best strategy for social change, this response was significantly more common among southern than northern respondents. Southern respondents' greater wariness toward proposals to create new global governance institutions may find its origin in the long history of southern representatives being marginalized within existing global governance institutions, such as the UN and WTO. Dominant conceptions of democracy are also associated with ideas developed within northern countries, which might also help to explain these findings.

These results parallel findings from the Democracy in Movement and the Mobilization of the Society (DEMOS) study of participants in the European Social Forum. There, more than 90 percent of activists reported that strengthening national governments deserved little or no attention. But there was not extensive support for a stronger European Union or United Nations either. Just 13 percent of respondents were very supportive of strengthening the EU, while 24 percent supported a stronger UN. In contrast, 70 percent of respondents supported the creation of entirely new institutions for global governance (della Porta et al. 2006).

Scales of Action and Global Democracy

Many analysts and observers stress the distinction between national- and international-level politics, and some might argue that the proliferation of more local and national forums, along with fewer WSFs, supports the case that national polities are the main arena for political mobilization. Yet the evolution of the WSF process suggests that the relationships between global and local politics are far more complex and interdependent. When civil society groups mobilize around international political arenas and norms, they do not necessarily compromise their ability to relate to local and national contexts. They may even strengthen their capacities to affect local practices through global-level activism and organizing. Discussions among activists about the tensions between local- and regional- or global-level organizing demonstrated strong commitments to both a local and global process. Organizers do not face a zero-sum competition in their decisions to focus on local- or global-level politics. In fact, a failure to understand how the global political context affects local settings and vice versa can lead to futile strategies.

Many activists in the WSF process recognize that local communities must be empowered both economically and politically, but they also know that this cannot happen without a fundamental reordering of global and national political institutions. Thus, many activists engage in multiple scales of action with little concern for where formal political and territorial boundaries lie (see, e.g., Stewart 2004). For instance, the campaign to "Reclaim the United Nations" demonstrates this:

> This strategy of mobilization should be developed at a variety of levels. There is no opposition between actions at the local level, national struggles for policy change, and initiatives on international institutions. All civil society work at a local,

national or regional level needs a change in the international system of governance. A more democratic functioning of international institutions would open up spaces for change at the national and local level. Implementing the principle of subsidiarity would restore decision making power for national and local democratic processes. Building new solidarities would strengthen the search for alternatives in countries of the South. (Tavola Della Pace 2005)

This need to build new solidarities is why the WSF process has evolved into a global series of loosely connected assemblies at a variety of scales. Because states are embedded in relationships with other states and international institutions (such as treaty bodies, international organizations like the UN, etc.), civil society groups cannot simply work to change the policies of individual states; they must also work to change the broader, interstate relationships and institutions that help define national interests and policies (see, e.g., Meyer et al. 1997). Problematically, existing political systems provide no real space for citizens to engage in thoughtful and informed debate about how the global political and economic system is organized.

Conclusion

The WSF process has helped fill that vacuum by creating democratic spaces where citizens can participate in debates about what policies might best serve the needs of their communities. It provides the *connective tissues* that link local and national political arenas with a global one. By participating in social forums, people learn how local realities are shaped by global policies and processes and by internationally circulated ideas and practices. Importantly, the WSF process contributes to the strengthening of transnational networks of activists that allow the stories of people in different countries to flow freely across highly diverse groups of people. This enables people to see the coincidences in how globalization affects people in similar social and economic circumstances. It also allows for local empowerment by facilitating the sharing of information about how communities in various places have resisted neoliberal economic globalization and countered other kinds of oppressive ideas, relations, and policies.

The WSF is the process of activists articulating and advancing their visions of a global order that are not limited to those made possible within other institutional spaces. By coming together in spaces that are largely autonomous from governments and international institutions such as the UN, activists have helped foster experimentation in new forms of global democracy, encouraging the development of skills, analyses, and identities that are essential to a democratic global polity. At the same time, they have generated autonomous initiatives to resist corporate-led globalization. These activities model a vision of the world that many activists in global justice movements hope to spread.

Aside from the various campaigns and change initiatives that it encourages, the WSF process serves as an important educational space. Here people learn about global politics and develop the global awareness and identities as well as the knowledge and skills needed to be active and engaged global citizens. They are challenged to consider how their local concerns relate to struggles in other parts of the world as they imagine themselves as part of a larger political community. In the various world, regional, and local social forums, people can cultivate resources and networks for acting in a global polity. Polletta refers to this as the "developmental benefits of participatory democracy" (2002). These contributions make the WSF process an important part of the effort to build a more democratic global order.

In short, although we might not yet have a truly global political system, the WSF process is an initiative of the global justice movement that clearly advances the globalization of politics. It does so by enabling people to imagine themselves as part of a global human community, even when the contexts within which people live reinforce local and national identities. Through the staging of local social forums that are linked to a globally integrated process, the WSF process fosters global identities and values while serving as an incubator for new ideas about how to address the world's problems. Moreover, its self-consciously polycentric nature, the diversity of actors it engages, and many participants' ideological aversion to traditional hierarchies and exclusions reproduce a culture of networked politics that Escobar (2004b) associates with "distributed intelligence." This kind of network structure, many argue, allows for more adaptation and innovation in response to an uncertain social and natural environment. On the one hand, it has allowed WSF activists to innovate solutions to problems as they arise in the course of engaging with the WSF process. On the other hand, such structures often fall short when coordinated action and follow-through are required.

Most importantly, the WSF process has expanded the possibilities for more and more people to be actively involved in discussions about what sort of world we want to build. By developing methods, such as those described above, to enhance the choices people have about how they make their living as well as how they engage in politics, social movements enhance the autonomy and self-sufficiency of local communities. Without such economic and political choices, the future of democracy is bleak. WSF participants have been modeling new forms of political action for democratic empowerment within local, national, and global contexts. And in the process they are helping find new ways of restructuring—and making more just and equitable—relations between men and women, between adults and children, and between groups differing in their nationality, race, or sexuality.

Chapter Six
CONCLUSION: THE WORLD SOCIAL FORUM PROCESS AND GLOBAL DEMOCRACY

The presentation of the World Social Forum process offered in this book provides readers with an introduction to one of the most novel forms of political organization in the contemporary era. From a single event in Porto Alegre, Brazil, in 2001 the WSF has expanded into "a permanent political and social process, punctuated with forum events. Its dynamics depend on building alternatives, proposals, projects, and campaigns between one forum and another" (http://www.wsfprocess.net). While the dynamism of the WSF is in part a response to the breadth and scope of political activism in a global era, the WSF thrives because there is a single and unifying demand voiced by social activists from different nations, political backgrounds, campaigns, and organizational forms that neoliberalism, or corporate globalization, must be changed. This expansive range of groups and individual WSF participants who are joined together with a singular focus generates the various creative tensions outlined in this book.

The diversity of actors and scales that constitute the WSF process complicates efforts to make the WSF a truly inclusive and open space for participants with varied cultural and political perspectives. Demonstrated quite clearly in this volume were tensions between horizontalism and verticalism, space as deliberative or conflictual, global versus local solutions, and even whether the social forum should emphasize itself as a space or an actor on the world stage. While our exploration of these issues presents key debates in the WSF, it also reveals the truly remarkable feature of the WSF: that it is able to contain and even grow from these tensions rather than succumb to internal discord. Diversity among WSF participants, coupled with a commitment to democratic principles, drives the forum to evolve, expand, and innovate.

"Prefigurative politics"—or the enactment of the world we envision—encapsulates the WSF process as a dynamic global entity. Social forum events are attempts to create miniworlds, models the forum process hopes to export around the globe. If thousands of committed activists from diverse movements with multiple visions of social change are able to come together and interact during and between forum events, the WSF is building a new model of global governance and civil society. In a sense, the success of the WSF helps make democratic globalization a reality.

Participants in the WSF realize, as Arendt understood, that public spaces can be multiple and do not necessarily have to surround the institutions of government. Publics spaces or, perhaps better said, counterpublics (Fraser 1992), can be created and exist elsewhere. The WSF, regional, and local forums reflect a counterpublic that—although spatially separated—is consistent with the sentiments that governance requires participation, humanity is for all of us to keep, and that the globe is not for sale.

We also have reviewed debates on the characterization of WSF space, concerns with exclusion and the need for wider and more diverse participation, and challenges to the decisionmaking process of the WSF itself. Yet, if we gauge democracy by the

extent of conflict, dissent, and dialogue, the WSF process represents a democratic success. Castoriadis, a modern Greek philoso-
pher, explains politics as the "self-responsible conscious collective action to alter a society's institutions that not only implies
but also presupposes the establishment of a public space open to
all who assert themselves as free and consider themselves and
each other as equals" (Curtis 1991:viii). Direct and participatory
democracy, or nonhierarchical decisionmaking, is highly
regarded as the method of choice by many organizations that
participate in the WSF and for the future world they envision.

Debates remain over whether and how to incorporate
political parties and governmental officials—many of whom
share the core values contained in the WSF Charter of Principles. And the WSF process has brought to the fore some important issues surrounding political strategy, with some participants
advocating approaches that engage existing political institutions
while others favor abandoning existing structures in favor of
more equitable and inclusive alternatives. The WSF process
seems to have responded to these tensions by becoming what
might be called a form of polycentric governance, or a transborder political body with an organizational architecture that
remains fluid, decentralized, and ever evolving.

The WSF process offers a fresh start for struggles *for* social
justice and human rights and *against* neoliberal capitalism.
Because the WSF is a *process* rather than an organization or an
event, it is by intention malleable in ways other international
bodies, like the United Nations, are not. Of course, these permanent institutions can change and have done so to include more
egalitarian practices, but this takes years of organizing, lobbying,
and politicking to institutionalize and even more time for this
change to be implemented. Activists who have struggled across
time and space for social justice in a host of causes—opposing
slavery and apartheid, for women's reproductive rights, in support

of environmental regulations, or in favor of lesbian, gay, bisexual, and transsexual rights—have often been told that social change takes time. But in the WSF process, many improvements are happening overnight, so to speak. In most cases, demands by participants who have identified unfairness in the WSF process are given immediate consideration and enacted upon. For instance, we saw in earlier chapters how protests against VIP spaces resulted in their abandonment and how the forum decisionmaking processes have been made more transparent.

Reaching a U.S. Audience

Although U.S.-based movements and organizations have taken part in past World Social Forums, there has been very little national-level coordination in their participation. Smaller city-based and regional forums have been held, such as the Boston Social Forum or the Midwest Social Forum, but the United States Social Forum (USSF) of 2007 is the first nationwide event, which many hope will lead to a sustained process of convergence. By providing an open space for collaboration, coordination, and exchange, the USSF has aimed to build a more united movement for peace and global justice in the United States, while respecting diversity and difference. This book went to press as the USSF convened, and so we draw from our understanding of the WSF process and our observations of the organizing process to date to offer our assessment of the key challenges and implications that will come from the USSF for social movement politics in the United States.

Held in Atlanta, Georgia, from June 27 to July 1, the USSF attracted wide interest from U.S. social movements and offered one of the first opportunities of horizontal open space exchange among these groups. As an original event on the U.S. political landscape and also an event that is not strictly homegrown but embedded in a global movement, the USSF holds great promise for politicizing Americans' understanding of their nation's relation to the globe. Although it is still too early to measure the impact of the U.S. Social Forum, we offer some thoughts based on our understanding and experience of the social forum process.

Chapter 2 shows that the forum's open space ideal reflects a horizontal networking logic characteristic of wider global justice movements and, on the other hand, that two competing views of what open space means have characterized the forum process: open space as deliberative space versus open space as agonistic space. These issues, and the associated conflicts and exclusions, were crucial in U.S.-based movements' preparations for the first USSF. At the same time, these dynamics take on particular dimensions given the unique political circumstances in the United States. With respect to the ideal of open space as deliberative space, the U.S. Social Forum will help diversify U.S.-based movements and networks for economic justice and peace and encourage them to find common ways of perceiving the challenges they confront as they form new alliances. Planning for the USSF has brought together a collection of organizations with no previous experience of working together, and it helped U.S. activists view their struggles as part of a broader, global process. Previous actions in Seattle, Washington, D.C., and elsewhere played this role, but their focus had been to critique rather than to build alternatives. Also, serious questions were raised about the lack of class and racial diversity in these earlier events. The WSF process emerged partly to enhance the inclusiveness of global protest events.

With regard to open space as agonistic space, we expect conflict to continue within and around the U.S. forum process. For example, as the first national event closes, will we see movements pushing for coordinated action, or will activists be satisfied with the process of discussion and debate experienced at the forum?

Will calls for a common platform or manifesto form around the USSF and will organizers and participants adhere to a strict interpretation of the Charter of Principles? In addition to deliberation versus action, there is the question of internal conflicts. What differences will we see emerging in the post-USSF years among organizers and participants? Will the division between horizontals and verticals that has characterized other forum processes find expression in the U.S. Social Forum? And will the opportunity to come together at the USSF help foster new understandings and unity among the diverse groups that make up U.S. civil society? We know from past forums that all deliberative spaces are also agonistic spaces, but the question remains as to what form such agonism will take in the U.S. context and to what consequence.

Grassroots movements and networks, including a large proportion of working-class people and activists of color, mainly led the organizing process of the USSF.[1] Several NGOs and NGO-based networks were also involved. The relationship between these groups and more direct action and/or anarchist-oriented groups will certainly be altered if the social forum process takes hold in the United States in upcoming years.

Perhaps the most important question relates to the issue of inclusion. One of the most widespread critiques of past U.S.-based global justice actions and networking processes has been the lack of diversity. Ever since the question "Where is the color in Seattle?" was raised, U.S. global justice activists have wrestled with the question of how to build a broad-based, grassroots movement for local and global justice led by those who are most affected, including working-class people and people of color. Organizers within the U.S. Social Forum process have made a concerted effort to ensure that groups representing these communities took a leading role in the process. Indeed, poverty reduction and people of color movements, such as Jobs with Justice, the Grassroots Global Justice Network, and the Southwest

Network for Economic and Environmental Justice, among many others, were at the forefront of the organizing effort. At this writing assessments are pending as to whether forum participants ultimately reflected this diversity, and if the U.S. Social Forum was a truly open space. To the extent that it succeeded, it can only help strengthen democracy in the United States and worldwide.

Finally, we continue to monitor if participants in the U.S. Social Forum espouse similarly radical ideas as their counterparts in the WSF and other regional social forums. Indeed, the prevailing ideological climate in the United States tends to be much more conservative than in other parts of the world, suggesting that the outcomes of the USSF might feature more reformist ideas and proposals. Within the world and other regional forums, some of the most antisystemic actors have worked within the WSF process while others have created their own autonomous spaces, contributing their radical visions regarding autonomy and self-management without necessarily taking part in the official forum. The question remains as to how these sectors engaged in the U.S. forum process. The success of the USSF in strengthening social movements greatly depends on efforts to publicize and distribute the ideas and action plans generated within and around it. Future research on the USSF will need to examine the mechanisms that will be created for publicizing and distributing the ideas and proposals that were generated within and around the U.S. Social Forum. Whether this takes the form of a project similar to the Mural of Proposals in Porto Alegre or an unofficial declaration on the part of participants, the success of the U.S. Social Forum will largely depend on the ability of organizers to spread the word about the myriad projects, ideas, and proposals generated by U.S. social movements.

Our interest in the WSF process and the USSF grows from our belief that these are fundamental to protecting the future of democracy that is based on social justice rather than formal elections. Historically, social movements have been essential to the democratization of national states, and today social movement actors and their allies are—consciously or not—strengthening possibilities for democracy in global institutions. Scholars exploring issues of democracy in global institutions identify the following criteria for assessing the impacts of particular social change efforts on global democratization (see, e.g., Glasius 2002). Effective efforts are:

- Enhancing *public awareness and debate* on global problems and proposals for their solution (e.g., cultivating a global "public sphere");
- Enhancing the *openness* and *representativeness* of international institutions by promoting access and giving voice to excluded groups and by diminishing power inequities among states;
- Enhancing *transparency* and accountability (both internally, among states, and externally, within the broader polity);
- Enhancing the *fairness* of global agreements based on shared principles of justice rather than on tradition, political expediency, or models of action;
- Enhancing the *effectiveness* of international law and institutions

In our view, the WSF process is contributing to each of these, although it can do more in this regard if participants become more self-aware of their roles as actors in the process of global democratization (see, e.g., Markoff 2005). Our analysis of the WSF has established how this process contributes to each of these, demonstrating its role as a democratizing force in today's world. Participants in the WSF process should recognize their essential role as global prodemocracy activists. They should be emboldened with the knowledge that they carry on the work of past democratizers. For their part, governments, political parties, and international agencies must recognize the vital need for citizen participation in global policymaking, and they can draw from the experience of the WSF to expand opportunities for such participation. Although we do not believe the WSF process should be institutionalized into a global parliament, we do believe that it can yield models of organization that can be useful for institutionalizing more democratic forms of global governance. Indeed, the WSF process should continue even as more formal institutions for democratic deliberation and accountability in world affairs are introduced.

The WSF process has had a tremendous political impact, notably in Latin America but also in India and Europe. But its impact should not be measured only by the changes happening at the level of national governments alone (which are quite momentous in a few cases), but also by those occurring in local-level government and in civil society. For instance, ideas promoted within the WSF process, such as municipal participatory budgeting, are being taken up in locations around the world. And the discourses of the forum find their way to the grassroots as activists returning from national, regional, and global meetings report back to their local communities on their experiences. Participation in the WSF process transforms organizations, groups, and individuals. They not only learn new ways to think about issues and their own place in a global society, but they also learn about democratic processes for addressing conflicts. People seeking a more democratic world can use and expand on the WSF process to make real the possibilities for global justice, sustainability, and peace. Indeed, not only is another world possible, it is already on the way.

Appendix:
WORLD SOCIAL FORUM
CHARTER OF PRINCIPLES

The committee of Brazilian organizations that conceived of, and organized, the first World Social Forum, held in Porto Alegre from January 25th to 30th, 2001, after evaluating the results of that Forum and the expectations it raised, consider it necessary and legitimate to draw up a Charter of Principles to guide the continued pursuit of that initiative. While the principles contained in this Charter—to be respected by all those who wish to take part in the process and to organize new editions of the World Social Forum—are a consolidation of the decisions that presided over the holding of the Porto Alegre Forum and ensured its success, they extend the reach of those decisions and define orientations that flow from their logic.

1. The World Social Forum is an open meeting place for reflective thinking, democratic debate of ideas, formulation of proposals, free exchange of experiences and interlinking for effective action, by groups and movements of civil society that are opposed to neoliberalism and to domination of the world by capital and any form of imperialism, and are committed to building a planetary society directed towards fruitful relationships among Humankind and between it and the Earth.

2. The World Social Forum at Porto Alegre was an event localized in time and place. From now on, in the certainty proclaimed at Porto Alegre that "another world is possible," it becomes a permanent process of seeking and building alternatives, which cannot be reduced to the events supporting it.

3. The World Social Forum is a world process. All the meetings that are held as part of this process have an international dimension.

4. The alternatives proposed at the World Social Forum stand in opposition to a process of globalization commanded by the large multinational corporations and by the governments and international institutions at the service of those corporations' interests, with the complicity of national governments. They are designed to ensure that globalization in solidarity will prevail as a new stage in world history. This will respect universal human rights, and those of all citizens—men and women—of all nations and the environment and will rest on democratic international systems and institutions at the service of social justice, equality and the sovereignty of peoples.

5. The World Social Forum brings together and interlinks only organizations and movements of civil society from all the countries in the world, but it does not intend to be a body representing world civil society.

6. The meetings of the World Social Forum do not deliberate on behalf of the World Social Forum as a body. No-one, therefore, will be authorized, on behalf of any of the editions of the Forum, to express positions claiming to be those of all its participants. The participants in the Forum shall not be called on to take decisions as a body, whether by vote or acclamation, on declarations or proposals for action that would commit all, or the majority, of them and that propose to be taken as establishing positions of the Forum as a body. It thus does not constitute a locus of power to be disputed by the participants in its meetings, nor does it intend to constitute the only option for interrelation and action by the organizations and movements that participate in it.

7. Nonetheless, organizations or groups of organizations that participate in the Forums' meetings must be assured the right, during such meetings, to deliberate on declarations or actions they may decide on, whether singly or in coordination with other participants. The World Social Forum undertakes to circulate such decisions widely by the means at its disposal, without directing, hierarchizing, censuring or restricting them, but as deliberations of the organizations or groups of organizations that made the decisions.

8. The World Social Forum is a plural, diversified, non-confessional, non-governmental and non-party context that, in a decentralized fashion, interrelates organizations and movements engaged in concrete action at levels from the local to the international to build another world.

9. The World Social Forum will always be a forum open to pluralism and to the diversity of activities and ways of engaging of the organizations and movements that decide to participate in it, as well as the diversity of genders, ethnicities, cultures, generations and physical capacities, providing they abide by this Charter of Principles. Neither party representations nor military organizations shall participate in the Forum. Government leaders and members of legislatures who accept the commitments of this Charter may be invited to participate in a personal capacity.

10. The World Social Forum is opposed to all totalitarian and reductionist views of economy, development and history and to the use of violence as a means of social control by the State. It upholds respect for Human Rights, the practices of real democracy, participatory democracy, peaceful relations, in equality and solidarity, among people, ethnicities, genders and peoples, and condemns all forms of domination and all subjection of one person by another.

11. As a forum for debate, the World Social Forum is a movement of ideas that prompts reflection, and the transparent circulation of the results of that reflection, on the mechanisms and instruments of domination by capital, on means and actions to resist and overcome that domination, and on the alternatives proposed to solve the problems of exclusion and social inequality that the process of capitalist globalization with its racist, sexist and environmentally destructive dimensions is creating internationally and within countries.

12. As a framework for the exchange of experiences, the World Social Forum encourages understanding and mutual recognition among its participant organizations and movements, and places special value on the exchange among them, particularly on all that society is building to center economic activity and political action on meeting the needs of people and respecting nature, in the present and for future generations.

13. As a context for interrelations, the World Social Forum seeks to strengthen and create new national and international links among organizations and movements of society, that—in both public and private life—will increase the capacity for nonviolent social resistance to the process of dehumanization the world is undergoing and to the violence used by the State, and reinforce the humanizing measures being taken by the action of these movements and organizations.

14. The World Social Forum is a process that encourages its participant organizations and movements to situate their actions, from the local level to the national level and seeking active participation in international contexts, as issues of planetary citizenship, and to introduce onto the global agenda the change-inducing practices that they are experimenting in building a new world in solidarity.

Approved and adopted in São Paulo, on April 9, 2001, by the organizations that make up the World Social Forum Organizing Committee, approved with modifications by the World Social Forum International Council on June 10, 2001.

Source: http://www.forumsocialmundial.org.br/main.php?id_menu=4&cd_language=2.

NOTES

Chapter One

1. "The 1972 Stockholm Conference institutionalized the environment as a legitimate concern of government, and it institutionalized NGOs as the instruments through which government could varnish its agenda with the appearance of public support. The primary outcome of the conference was a recommendation to create the United Nations Environment Programme (UNEP) which became a reality in 1973" (Lamb 1997).

Chapter Two

1. Research on the European Social Forums reveals intense debates on two main dimensions: delegation versus direct democracy, and majority rule versus consensus. Half of the sample of 244 European global justice organizations adopted an *associational* conception of internal decisionmaking, in the sense that—at least formally—they follow a model based on delegation of power and majority principle. Overall, almost two-fifths of the organizations fall in the deliberative representative category, where the principle of consensus is mixed with

the principle of delegation; almost one-third of the groups adopt an associational model that is based on majoritarian vote and delegation; around one-fifth of the groups bridge a consensual decisionmaking method with the principle of participation (deliberative participative model) (della Porta and Mosca 2006).

2. "Summit hopping" refers to the practice of mobilizing mass protests at the various sites of intergovernmental meetings of the World Bank, WTO, etc.

3. Arendt's work, however, was always cast within the context of the state.

4. Some refer to a rupture between the forum as a space and the forum as a movement. However, *movement* means very different things in different places. In parts of Latin America, for example, *movement* refers to a highly organized collective actor with a clear leadership structure that makes decisions and has a grassroots base. The Landless Workers in Brazil (MST) follow this model, for example. In other parts of the world, however, such as the United States and Europe, *movement* refers to a much more diffuse political actor involving multiple groups and organizations. To avoid this confusion here we thus refer to the tension between the forum as a space and the forum as an actor.

5. The text is archived at www.zmag.org/sustainers/content/ 2005-02/20group_of_nineteen.cfm.

6. The appeal and other materials are archived at www.open spaceforum.net/twiki/tiki-index.php?page=Bamakoappeal, accessed July 23, 2006.

7. The discussion of autonomous spaces draws on Juris (2008).

Chapter Three

1. Also, in 2006 the three polycentric meetings were held in the global south, in Pakistan, Mali, and Venezuela.

2. For the 2005 survey instrument see http://www.irows.ucr.edu/ research/tsmstudy.htm.

3. The apparent lack of attendance from Canada in Figure 3.1 is due to those attending coming from cities that border the United States. Eighteen of our respondents were from Canada, representing 2.8 percent of the total number of respondents mapped.

4. Fundação Perseu Abramo's survey of participants was conducted during the 2001 meeting in Porto Alegre; IBASE's survey was carried out during the 2005 WSF in Porto Alegre, Brazil. IBASE (2006) found an even higher share, or 80 percent, of respondents to their survey of WSF participants were from Brazil.

5. Quilombos were communities of resistance where Afro-Brazil-ian slaves ran away to and developed their own alternative collective and spiritually based forms of social organization together with small groups of indigenous people and some Euro-Brazilians.

6. See report by Elsa Duhagon archived at www.choike.org/nuevo_eng/informes/2598.html, retrieved on January 12, 2007.

7. However, since 85 percent of respondents claimed that they had participated in a public demonstration or protest at least once in the past year, these figures might actually underestimate the extent of social movement participation among WSF participants. Some survey respondents apparently skipped this question, which came at the end of a long survey.

8. This compares with 46 percent who indicated trust in local governments, 15 percent in national parliaments, 27 percent in the European Union, and 30 in the United Nations (see della Porta et al. 2006).

9. For example, in December 2006 representatives of the political party Movimiento al Socialismo (MAS) from Bolivia were actively involved in the organization of the subregional social forum on regional integration in Cochabamba, Bolivia.

10. For example, critics charge that the format and size of plenary sessions and workshops reinforce the power of celebrity activists and intellectuals and stifle dialogue and active participation among those attending the WSF. Others point to the lack of transparent decision-making by nonelected and exclusive decisionmaking bodies (i.e., the Organizing Council and the International Council). Other critics charge that the WSF has been co-opted by mainstream NGOs and unions and through reliance on government and corporate funding

and support. Other criticisms have led to increased efforts to practice ecological sustainability and participatory economics within the WSF and to pay greater attention to issues affecting people of color and women (Byrd 2005:159; Patomaki and Teivainen 2004; Smith 2004c).

Chapter Four

1. The statistical significance of the relationship between anticapitalist views and each of these factors was less than or equal to 0.05 except for union membership, which was statistically significant at the 0.10 level.

2. These percentages refer to valid percentages (i.e., of those who answered the question). About 8 percent of respondents did not answer this question.

3. Dumping occurs when one country exports a significant amount of goods to another country at prices much lower than in the domestic market.

4. The complete 2005 edition of the WSF Mural of Proposals can be found at www.memoriaviva.org/fsm05/indexen.htm, accessed January 4, 2007.

5. GNU stands for GNU is Not Unix (Caruso 2005:173).

Chapter Five

1. Some thematic and regional forums are "officially" part of the social forum process, while others simply use the forum name but are not officially endorsed by the IC. This relates to a long-standing debate in the IC over whether the forum is more like a franchise or a public domain. Some members see the forum as a franchise, in which those who wanted to organize a forum can do so, but would have to "apply," so to speak, to the IC for official recognition. Others see the forum as existing in the public domain, and thus anyone can organize a forum whenever and however they like, so long as they respect the Charter of Principles. Ultimately a compromise has been reached: some regional and thematic

forums are officially endorsed by the IC, while others use the forum name, but have no official connection to the process. This distinction is still reflected on the WSF website.

2. European Social Forums have drawn 60,000 in Florence (2002), 70,000 in Paris (2003), 50,000 in London (2004), and 35,000 in Athens (2006).

3. Although they remain formally independent from the WSF's International Council, many organizers working to host local social forums are familiar with or have participated in one or more regional or world forums, and in cases like the U.S. social forum, representatives of the local organizing committee are in dialogue with the WSF International Council in the course of their planning and post-forum organizing. Local social forums agree to the Charter of Principles of the WSF but are otherwise free to organize events in ways that suit local contexts.

4. While U.S. activists have been attending the world gatherings in larger numbers in more recent years, the WSF process has still not taken root in U.S. social movements, as is witnessed by the relatively late and limited local- and national-level organizing around the WSF process.

5. Identifying local social forums is complicated by the fact that not all local forums use the Internet to publicize their events, as this medium is less important to local organizing efforts. Also, websites of local forums are not typically sustained for long periods after the events. We drew from Internet traces of these events, researcher notes, interviews with activists, and the work of Glasius and Timms (2006) to compile this list.

6. Rupp found a similar pattern in early transnational women's organizing (1997).

7. The summary of local economic initiatives draws from Jackie Smith (2006).

8. For more on community currency initiatives, see Kent (2005).

9. The UN Norms for Business have already been adopted by the UN Sub-Commission on the Promotion and Protection of Human Rights, a first step in achieving a binding international treaty.

10. See, e.g., http://reclaimdemocracy.org/personhood/#campaign.

11. We differentiated respondents from the global north and south based on information on their gross national income per capita in 2004 of the respondents' country of residence (World Bank 2006; see also www.worldbank.org/data/). We used the World Bank's classification of "high income" to identify countries in the north and considered all other countries to be in the south. The percentages in Tables 5.3 and 5.4 refer to "valid percentages," or the percentages of those who actually answered the question or chose one response.

12. Differences in respondents' views across world system position are statistically significant at the .05 level.

Chapter Six

1. The WSF IC made a deliberate decision to designate this segment of U.S. social movements as the core organizing committee for the USSF in order to strengthen participation from these underrepresented groups.

REFERENCES

Alvarez, Sonia, Nalu Faria, and Miriam Nobre. 2004. "Another (Also Feminist) World Is Possible: Constructing Transnational Spaces and Global Alternatives from the Movements." Pp. 199–206 in *World Social Forum: Challenging Empires*, edited by Jai Sen, Anita Anand, Arturo Escobar, Peter Waterman. New Delhi: Viveka.

Amin, Samir, Anne Peeters, and Denis Stokkink. 2002. *Mondialisation: Comprendre pour agir*. Paris: Éditions Complexe.

Amnesty International. 2004. "The UN Human Rights Norms for Business: Towards Legal Accountability." Paper distributed at ESF, London, Amnesty International.

Arendt, Hannah. 1958. *The Human Condition*. Chicago: University of Chicago Press.

———. 1982. *Lectures on Kant's Political Philosophy*. Chicago: University of Chicago Press.

———. 1993. "What Is Freedom?" Pp. 143–171 in *Between Past and Future: Eight Exercises in Political Thought*. London: Penguin.

Arrighi, Giovanni, Terence K. Hopkins, and Immanuel Wallerstein. 1989. *Antisystemic Movements*. London: Verso.

Articulation Feminista Marcosur. 2005. "Noticia Forummentalismos: Las Contradicciones del Forum Social Mundial." Retrieved July 17, 2006 (www.choike.org/nuevo/informes/2554.html).

Ayres, Jeffrey M. 1998. *Defying Conventional Wisdom.* Toronto: University of Toronto Press.

Babb, Sarah. 2003. "The IMF in Sociological Perspective: A Tale of Organizational Slippage." *Studies in Comparative International Development* 38:3–27.

Bandy, Joe. 2000. "Bordering the Future: Resisting Neoliberalism in the Borderlands." *Critical Sociology* 26:232–267.

Becker, Marc. 2003. "Another World Is Possible." *Net-works News, Newsletter of the Wisconsin Network for Peace and Justice* 13(4):1, 9.

———. 2005. "Hugo Chavez Returns to the World Social Forum." Retrieved December 7, 2006 (http://www.yachana.org/reports/wsf5/chavez.html).

———. 2007. "World Social Forum." *Peace and Change* 32(2):203–220.

Bello, W. 2000. "2000: The Year of Global Protest Against Globalization" (www.nadir.org/nadir/initiativ/agp/free/bello/2000global_protest.htm).

Benasayag, Miguel, and Diego Sztulwark. 2002. *Du contre-pouvoir.* Paris: La Découverte.

Biccum, April. 2005. "The World Social Forum: Exploiting the Ambivalence of 'Open' Spaces." *Ephemera* 5(2):116–133.

Boli, John, and George M. Thomas, eds. 1999. *Constructing World Culture: International Nongovernmental Organizations Since 1875.* Stanford: Stanford University Press.

Boswell, Terry, and Christopher Chase-Dunn. 2000. *The Spiral of Capitalism and Socialism: Toward Global Democracy.* Boulder, Colo.: Lynne Rienner.

Brunelle, Dorval. 2006. "Le Forum social mondial: Origine et participants." *Observatoire des Amériques* (http://www.ameriques.uqam.ca).

———. 2007. *From World Order to Global Disorder: States, Markets, and Dissent.* Vancouver: University of British Columbia Press.

Burbach, R. 1994. "Roots of the Postmodern Rebellion in Chiapas." *New Left Review* 1:205.

Byrd, Scott C. 2005. "The Porto Alegre Consensus: Theorizing the Forum Movement." *Globalizations* 2(1):151–163.

Carlsson, Ingvar, and Shridath Ramphal. 1995. "Co-chairmen's Foreword." Pp. xii–xv in *Our Global Neighborhood: Report of the Com-*

mission on Global Governance, by the Commission on Global Governance. New York: Oxford University Press.

Caruso, Giuseppe. 2005. "Open Office and Free Software." *Ephemera* 5(2):173–192.

Cassen, Bernard. 2006. "The World Social Forum: Where Do We Stand and Where Are We Going?" Pp. 79–83 in *Global Civil Society 2005/6*, edited by Marlies Glasius, Mary Kaldor, Helmut Anheier. London: Sage Publications.

Cavanagh, John, and Jerry Mander, eds. 2002. *Alternatives to Economic Globalization: A Better World Is Possible,* 2nd ed. San Francisco: Berrett-Koehler Publishers.

Chase-Dunn, Christopher, Ellen Reese, Mark Herkenrath, Rebecca Alvarez, Erika Gutierriez, and Christine Petit. 2008. "North-South Contradictions and Bridges at the World Social Forum." In *North and South in the World Political Economy*, edited by Rafael Reuveny and William R. Thompson. Cambridge, Mass.: Blackwell.

Cleaver, Harry M. 1995. "The Zapatistas and the Electronic Fabric of Struggle." Retrieved March 18, 2004 (www.eco.utexas.edu/faculty/Cleaver/zaps.html).

Cohen, Jean L. 1985. "Strategy or Identity." *Social Research* 52:663–716.

Commission on Global Governance. 1995. *Our Global Neighborhood: Report of the Commission on Global Governance.* New York: Oxford University Press.

Conway, Janet. 2004. "Citizenship in a Time of Empire: The World Social Forum as a New Public Space." *Citizenship Studies* 8(4): 367–381.

Crozier, Michel, Samuel P. Huntington, and Joji Watanuki. 1975. *The Crisis of Democracy: Report on the Governability of Democracies to the Trilateral Commission.* New York: New York University Press.

Curtis, David. A. 1991. "Foreword." Pp. v–x in *Philosophy, Politics, and Autonomy: Essays in Political Philosophy* by Cornelius Castoriadis. Oxford: Oxford University Press.

De Angelis. Massimo. 2005. "PR Like Process!" *Ephemera* 5(2): 193–204.

della Porta, Donatella. 2001. *I partiti politici.* Bologna: Il Mulino.

————. 2007. *Conceptions and Practice of Democracy in the European Social Forums.* WP5 Report, Democracy in Movement and the Mobilization of the Society—DEMOS (http://demos.iue.it/).

della Porta, Donatella, Massimiliano Andretta, Lorenzo Mosca, and Herbert Reiter. 2006. *Globalization from Below: Transnational Activists and Protest Networks.* Minneapolis: University of Minnesota Press.

della Porta, Donatella, and Lorenzo Mosca, eds. 2006. *Organizational Networks: Organizational Structures and Practices of Democracy.* WP4 Report, Democracy in Movement and the Mobilization of the Society—DEMOS (http://demos.iue.it/).

della Porta, Donatella, and Herbert Reiter, eds. 2006. *Organizational Ideology and Vision of Democracy in the Global Justice Movement.* WP3 Report, Democracy in Movement and the Mobilization of the Society—DEMOS (http://demos.iue.it/).

Diani, Mario. 1995. *Green Networks.* Edinburgh: Edinburgh University Press.

Doerr, Nicole. 2005. "Towards a European Public Sphere Beyond Language Barriers? The Case of the European Social Forum." Paper presented at the third general session of the European Consortium for Political Research. September 8–10, 2005, Budapest.

Dowling, Emma. 2005. "The Ethics of Engagement Revisited." *Ephemera* 5(2):205–215.

Eschle, Catherine, and Bice Maiguascha. 2005. "Research in Progress: Making Feminist Sense of 'the Anti-Globalisation Movement.'" *Ephemera* 5(2):216–220.

Escobar, Arturo. 2004a. "Beyond the Third World: Imperial Globality, Global Coloniality and Anti-Globalisation Social Movements." *Third World Quarterly* 25(1):207–230.

————. 2004b. "Other Worlds Are (Already) Possible: Self-Organisation, Complexity, and Post-Capitalist Cultures." Pp. 349–358 in *Challenging Empires: The World Social Forum*, edited by Jai Sen, Anita Anand, Arturo Escobar, Peter Waterman. New Delhi: Viveka.

Evans, Peter B. 1997. "The Eclipse of the State? Reflections on Stateness in an Era of Globalization." *World Politics* 50:62–87.

Fraser, Nancy. 1992. "Rethinking the Public Sphere." In *Habermas and the Public Sphere*, edited by Craig Calhoun. Cambridge: MIT Press.

Freeman, Jo. 1974. "The Tyranny of Structurelessness," Pp. 202–214 in *Women in Politics*, edited by Jane Jaquette. New York: John Wiley.

Gerhards, J., and D. Rucht. 1992. "Mesomobilization." *American Journal of Sociology* 8:555–595.

Gibson-Graham, J. K. 2006. *A Postcapitalist Politics*. Minneapolis: University of Minnesota Press.

Gill, S. 2000. "Toward a Postmodern Prince? The Battle in Seattle as a Moment in the New Politics of Globalisation." *Millennium: Journal of International Studies* 29(1):131–140.

Glasius, Marlies. 2002. "Expertise in the Cause of Justice: Global Civil Society Influence on the Statute for an International Criminal Court." Pp. 137–169 in *Global Civil Society Yearbook, 2002*, edited by M. Glasius, M. Kaldor, and H. Anheier. Oxford: Oxford University Press.

Glasius, Marlies, and Jill Timms. 2006. "The Role of Social Forums in Global Civil Society: Radical Beacon or Strategic Infrastructure." Pp. 190–239 in *Global Civil Society Yearbook, 2005/6*, edited by M. Glasius, M. Kaldor, and H. Anheier. Thousand Oaks, Calif.: Sage.

Guay, Nathalie. 2005. "La jeunesse dans le mouvement altermondialiste: Marginalization ou auto-exclusion?" *Observatoire des Amériques* (http://www.ameriques.uqam.ca).

Guru, Gopal. 2004. "Dalit Vision of India." *Futures* 36(6/7):757–763.

Habermas, Jürgen. 1992. "Further Reflections on the Public Sphere." Pp. 421–461 in *Habermas and the Public Sphere*, edited by Craig Calhoun. Cambridge, Mass.: MIT Press.

———. 1996. "Three Normative Models of Democracy." Pp. 21–31 in *Democracy and Difference*, edited by Seyla Benhabib. Princeton: Princeton University Press.

Halliday, F. 2000. "Getting Real About Seattle." *Millennium: Journal of International Studies* 29(1):123–129.

Harvey, Neil. 1998. *The Chiapas Rebellion: The Struggle for Land and Democracy*. Durham: Duke University Press.

Held, David, and Anthony McGrew. 2002. *Globalization/Antiglobalization*. Cambridge: Polity.

IBASE (Brazilian Institute of Social and Economic Analyses). 2006. "Study of Participants at the 2005 WSF." Retrieved January 5, 2007

(www.ibase.org.br/userimages/relatorio_fsm2005_INGLES2
.pdf).

International Network for Economic, Social, and Cultural Rights.
2005. "History of UN Norms for Business Campaign." Retrieved
March 8, 2007 (http://www.orgitecture.com/escr/actions_more/
actions_more_show.htm?doc_id=430993).

Juris, Jeffrey S. 2004. "Networked Social Movements: The Network
Society." Pp. 341–362 in *The Network Society*, edited by Manuel
Castells. London: Edward Elgar.

————. 2005a. "The New Digital Media and Activist Networking
Within Anti-Corporate Globalization Movements." *The Annals of
the American Academy of Political and Social Sciences* 597:189–208.

————. 2005b. "Social Forums and Their Margins: Networking Logics and the Cultural Politics of Autonomous Space." *Ephemera*
5(2):253–272.

————. 2008. *Networking Futures: The Movements Against Corporate
Globalization*. Durham, N.C.: Duke University Press.

Kaldor, M. 2000. "Civilising Globalisation? The Implications of the
'Battle in Seattle.'" *Millennium: Journal of International Studies* 29(1):
105–114.

Karides, Marina. 2007. "Feminist Contentions at the WSF." In *World-
Systemic Crisis and Contending Political Scenarios*, edited by Joya Misra
and Agustin Lao-Montes. Boulder, Colo.: Paradigm Publishers.

Karides, Marina, and Mark Frezzo. 2006. "A Commentary on the WSF
and the Social Forum Movement." (http://www.sociologists
withoutborders.org/documents/kar_frez_wsf.pdf).

Kellner, Douglas. 2000. "Habermas, the Public Sphere, and Democracy:
A Critical Intervention." Pp. xi–xv in *Perspectives on Habermas*,
edited by Lewis Hahn. La Salle, Ill.: Open Court Press.

Kent, Deirdre. 2005. *Healthy Money, Healthy Planet: Developing Sustainability Through New Money Systems*. Nelson, New Zealand: Craig
Potton Publishing.

Kenworthy, Lane. 1995. *In Search of National Economic Success: Balancing
Competition and Cooperation*. Thousand Oaks, Calif.: Sage.

Khasnabish, Alex. 2005. "'You Will No Longer Be You, Now You Are
Us': Zapitismo, Transnational Activism, and the Political Imagina-

tion." PhD diss., Department of Anthropology, McMaster University, Hamilton, Ontario.

King, Jamie. 2004. "The Packet Gang." *Metamute* 27. Retrieved April 13, 2005 (http://info.interactivist.net/article.pl?sid=04/01/30/1158224&mode=nested&tid=9).

Klak, Thomas, and Dennis Conway. 1998. "From Neoliberalism to Sustainable Development." Pp. 257–277 in *Globalization and Neoliberalism: The Caribbean Context,* edited by T. Klak. Lanham, Md.: Rowman and Littlefield.

Klein, Naomi. 2002. *Fences and Windows: Dispatches from the Front Lines of the Globalization Debate.* London: Flamingo.

Kull, Steven, Clay Ramsay, and Evan Lewis. 2003. "Misperceptions, the Media, and the Iraq War." *Political Science Quarterly* 118:569–598.

Lamb, Henry. 1997. *Maurice Strong: The New Guy in Your Future!* (http://www.sovereignty.net/p/sd/strong.html).

Macdonald, Laura. 2005. "Gendering Transnational Social Movement Analysis: Women's Groups Contest Free Trade in the Americas." Pp. 21–42 in *Coalitions Across Borders: Negotiating Difference and Unity in Transnational Coalitions Against Neoliberalism,* edited by J. Bandy and J. Smith. Lanham, Md.: Rowman and Littlefield.

Manoharan, Vincent. 2004. Interview by P. J. Smith, November, Mumbai, India.

Markoff, John. 1999. "Globalization and the Future of Democracy." *Journal of World-Systems Research* 5:242–262 (http://csf.colorado.edu/wsystems/jwsr.html).

———. 2005. "Essential Contestants, Essential Contests." Unpublished manuscript, University of Pittsburgh.

McMichael, Philip. 2003. *Development and Social Change: A Global Perspective.* 3d ed. Thousand Oaks, Calif.: Pine Forge.

Meyer, John W., John Boli, George M. Thomas, and Francisco O. Ramirez. 1997. "World Society and the Nation-State." *American Journal of Sociology* 103:144–181.

Milan, Stefania. 2005. "Communication: Open Systems for Open Politics." Retrieved January 4, 2007 (www.ipsterraviva.net/tv/wsf2005/viewstory.asp?idnews=77).

Miller, Ethan. 2006. "Other Economies Are Possible: Organizing Toward an Economy of Cooperation and Solidarity." *Dollars and*

Sense, September 9 (http://www.dollarsandsense.org/archives/2006/0706emiller.html).

Moghadam, Valentine. 2005. *Globalizing Women: Transnational Feminist Networks.* Baltimore: Johns Hopkins University Press.

Mouffe, Chantal. 1999. "Deliberative Democracy or Agonistic Pluralism?" *Social Research* 66.

Munck, Ronaldo. 2002. "Globalization and Democracy: A New 'Great Transformation'?" *The Annals of the American Academy of Political and Social Science: Globalization and Democracy* 581:10–21.

Nineham, Chris, and Alex Callinicos. 2005. "Critical Reflections on the Fifth World Social Forum." Woods Hole, Mass.: Znet. Retrieved December 14, 2006 (http://www.zmag.org/content/print_article.cfm?itemID=7197&sectionID=1).

Notes from Nowhere. 2003. *We Are Everywhere.* London: Verso.

Nunes, Rodrigo. 2005. "The Intercontinental Youth Camp as the Unthought of the World Social Forum." *Ephemera* 5(2):277–296.

Olesen, Thomas. 2005. *International Zapatismo.* London: Zed Books.

Osterweil, Michal. 2004a. "A Cultural-Political Approach to Reinventing the Political." *International Social Science Journal* 56(182): 495–506.

———. 2004b. "De-centering the Forum." Pp. 183–191 in *Challenging Empires,* edited by Jai Sen, Anita Anand, Arturo Escobar, Peter Waterman. New Delhi: Viveka.

Patomaki, Heikki, and Tevio Teivainen. 2004. *A Possible World: Democratic Transformation of Global Institutions.* London: Zed Books.

———. 2006. "Epilogue: Beyond the Political Party/Civil Society Dichotomy." Working Paper 1/2006. Pp. 180–188 in *Democratic Politics Globally: Elements for a Dialogue on Global Political Party Formations,* edited by Katarina Sehm-Patomaki and Marko Ulvila. Helsinki, Finland: Network Institute for Global Democratization.

Peet, Richard. 2003. *Unholy Trinity: The IMF, World Bank, and WTO.* New York: Zed Books.

Pleyers, Geoffrey. 2004. "The Social Forums as an Ideal Model of Convergence." *International Journal of the Social Sciences* 182:507–519.

Polletta, Francesca. 2002. *Freedom Is an Endless Meeting.* Chicago: University of Chicago Press.

Portes, Alejandro. 1997. "Neo-liberalism and the Sociology of Development: Emerging Trends and Unanticipated Facts." *Population and Development Review* 23:2–25.

Ray, Kiely. 1998. "The Crisis of Global Development." Pp. 24–44 in *Globalization and the Third World*, edited by Kiely Ray and P. Marfleet. London: Routledge.

Reese, Ellen, Christopher Chase-Dunn, Mark Herkenrath, Rebecca Giem, Erika Guttierriez, and Christine Petit. 2006. "Alliances and Divisions Within the 'Movement of Movements': Survey Findings from the 2005 World Social Forum." Paper presented at the 2006 annual meeting of the American Sociological Association meeting in Montreal, Canada.

Rice, Andrew E., and Cyril Ritchie. 1995. "Relationships Between International Non-Governmental Organizations and the United Nations: A Research and Policy Paper." *Transnational Associations* 47(5):254–265. (http://www.uia.org/uiadocs/unngos.htm).

Robinson, William. 2004. *A Theory of Global Capitalism*. Baltimore, Md.: Johns Hopkins University Press.

Ronfeldt, David F., John Arquilla, Graham Fuller, and Melissa Fuller. 1998. *The Zapatista "Social Netwar" in Mexico*. Santa Monica, Calif.: Rand.

Routledge, Paul. 2004. "Convergence of Commons." *The Commoner* (Autumn/Winter). Retrieved April 13, 2005 (www.thecommoner. org).

Rucht, Dieter. 2000. "Distant Issue Movements in Germany: Empirical Description and Theoretical Reflections." Pp. 76–107 in *Globalizations and Social Movements: Culture, Power, and the Transnational Public Sphere*, edited by J. A. Guidry, M. D. Kennedy, and M. N. Zald. Ann Arbor: University of Michigan Press.

Rupp, Leila J. 1997. *Worlds of Women: The Making of an International Women's Movement*. Princeton, N.J.: Princeton University Press.

Scholte, J. A. 2000. "Cautionary Reflections on Seattle." *Millennium: Journal of International Studies* 29(1):115–121.

Schönleitner, Günter. 2003. "World Social Forum: Making Another World Possible?" Pp. 127–149 in *Globalizing Civic Engagement: Civil Society and Transnational Action*, edited by John Clark. London: Earthscan.

Schultz, Markus S. 1998. "Collective Action Across Borders: Opportunity Structures, Network Capacities, and Communicative Praxis in the Age of Advanced Globalization." *Sociological Perspectives* 41:587–617.

Sehm-Patomaki, Katarina, and Marko Ulvila, eds. 2006. *Democratic Politics Globally: Elements for a Dialogue on Global Political Party Formations.* Working Paper 1/2006. Helsinki, Finland: Network Institute for Global Democratization.

Seoane, J., and E. Taddei. 2002. "From Seattle to Porto Alegre: The Anti-Neoliberal Globalization Movement." *Current Sociology* 50(1):99–122.

Sikkink, Kathryn. 1986. "Codes of Conduct for Transnational Corporations: The Case of the WHO/UNICEF Code." *International Organization* 40:815–840.

Sklar, Holly, ed. 1980. *Trilateralism: The Trilateral Commission and Elite Planning for World Management.* Montreal: Black Rose Books.

Smith, Jackie. 2002. "Globalizing Resistance: The Battle of Seattle and the Future of Social Movements." Pp. 183–199 in *Globalization and Resistance: Transnational Dimensions of Social Movements*, edited by J. Smith and H. Johnston. Lanham, Md.: Rowman and Littlefield.

―――. 2004a. "Exploring Connections Between Global Integration and Political Mobilization." *Journal of World Systems Research* 10: 255–285.

―――. 2004b. "The World Social Forum and the Challenges of Global Democracy." *Global Networks* 4(4):413–421.

―――. 2005. "The Struggle for Global Society in a World System." Public Sociologies Essay, *Social Forces* 83(3):1279–1285.

―――. 2006. "Perspectives: Do Social Movements Offer Viable Alternatives?" *Kasarinlan: Philippine Journal of Third World Studies* 21(2):152–157.

―――. 2008. *Global Visions, Rival Networks: Social Movements for Global Democracy.* Baltimore, Md.: Johns Hopkins University Press.

Smith, Peter J., and Elizabeth Smythe. 2001. "Globalization, Citizenship, and Technology." In *Culture and Politics in the Information Age*, edited by Frank Webster. London: Routledge.

Starr, Amory. 2005. *Global Revolt*. London: Zed Books.

Starr, Amory, and Jason Adams. 2004. "Anti-globalization." *New Political Science* 25(1):19–42.

Sternbach, Nancy Saporta, Marysa Navarro-Aranguren, Patricia Chuchryk, and Sonia E. Alvarez. 1992. "Feminisms in Latin America: From Bogota to San Bernardo." Pp. 207–239 in *The Making of Social Movements in Latin America: Identity, Strategy, and Democracy*, edited by A. Escobar and S. E. Alvarez. Boulder: Westview.

Stewart, Julie. 2004. "When Local Troubles Become Transnational: The Transformation of a Guatemalan Indigenous Rights Movement." *Mobilization* 9:259–278.

Tavola Della Pace. 2005. "Reclaim Our UN." Porto Alegre, Brazil.

Teivainen, Teivo. 2002. "The World Social Forum and Global Democratisation: Learning from Porto Alegre." *Third World Quarterly* 23(4):621–632.

———. 2004a. "Twenty-two Theses on the Problems of Democracy in the World Social Forum." *Transform!* 1. Retrieved April 19, 2004 (http://www.transform.it/newsletter/news_transform01.html).

———. 2004b. "The WSF: Arena or Actor?" Pp. 122–130 in *Challenging Empires*, edited by Jai Sen, Anita Anand, Arturo Escobar, Peter Waterman. New Delhi: Viveka.

———. 2006. "WSF 2009: Dilemmas of Decision-Making on the Periodicity of the Forums." *Network Institute for Global Democratization*. Retrieved January 3, 2007 (http://www.nigd.org/nan/nan-doc-store/10-2006/wsf-2009-dilemmas-of-decision-making-on-the-periodicity-of-the-forums).

UNDP. 2005. *Human Development Report 2005: International Cooperation at a Crossroads*. New York: Oxford.

U.S. Census Bureau, International Data Base. 2006. (www.census.gov/ipc/www/idbnew.html).

Vargas, Gina. 2004. "The WSF and Tensions in the Construction of Global Alternative Thinking." Pp. 228–232 in *Challenging Empires: The World Social Forum*, edited by Jai Sen, Anita Anand, Arturo Escobar, Peter Waterman. New Delhi: Viveka.

Vázquez, R. 2006. "Thinking the Event with Hannah Arendt." *European Journal of Social Theory* 9(1):43–57.

Vera-Zavala, America. 2004. "The World Women's Forum." Retrieved July 17, 2006 (www.countercurrents.org/gender-zavala310104).

Verba, Sidney, Kay Schlozman, and Henry Brady. 1995. *Voice and Equality: Civic Volunteerism in American Politics.* Cambridge: Harvard University Press.

Wainwright, Hilary. 2003. *Reclaim the State.* London: Verso.

———. 2004. "The Forum as Jazz." Pp. xvii–xx in *Challenging Empires: The World Social Forum,* edited by Jai Sen, Anita Anand, Arturo Escobar, Peter Waterman. New Delhi: Viveka.

Walton, John, and David Seddon. 1994. *Free Markets and Food Riots: The Politics of Global Adjustment.* Cambridge, Mass.: Blackwell.

Warner, Michael. 2002. "Publics and Counterpublics." *Public Culture* 14(1):49–90.

Waterman, Peter. 2002. "What's Left Internationally?" Institute of Social Studies, The Hague, Working Series 362. Retrieved May 19, 2004 (http://groups/yahoo.com/groups/GoSoDia).

———. 2004. "The World Social Forum and the Global Justice and Solidarity Movement: A Backgrounder." Pp. 55–66 in *Challenging Empires: The World Social Forum,* edited by Jai Sen, Anita Anand, Arturo Escobar, Peter Waterman. New Delhi: Viveka.

———. 2005. "Talking Across Difference in an Interconnected World of Labour." Pp. 141–162 in *Coalitions Across Borders: Transnational Protest and the Neoliberal Order,* edited by J. Bandy and J. Smith. Boulder, Colo.: Rowman and Littlefield.

Waterman, Peter, and Jill Timms. 2004. "Trade Union Internationalism and a Global Civil Society in the Making." Pp. 175–202 in *Global Civil Society 2004/5,* edited by Marlies Glasius, Helmut Anheier, and Mary Kaldor. London: Sage.

Whitaker, Chico. 2004. "The WSF as Open Space." Pp. 111–121 in *World Social Forum: Challenging Empires,* edited by Jai Sen, Anita Anand, Arturo Escobar, Peter Waterman. New Delhi: Viveka.

———. 2006. "The World Social Forum: Where Do We Stand and Where Are We Going?" Pp. 66–72 in *Global Civil Society Yearbook 2005/6,* edited by Marlies Glasius, Mary Kaldor, and Helmut Anheier. Thousand Oaks, Calif.: Sage.

Williamson, John. 1997. "The Washington Consensus Revisited." Pp. 48–61 in *Economic and Social Development into the XXI Century,* edited by Louis Emmerij. Baltimore, Md.: Johns Hopkins University Press.

World Bank. 2006. *World Development Report.* New York: Oxford University Press. WSF (World Social Forum). 2001. "Charter of Principles." Retrieved April 13, 2005 (http://www.forumsocialmundial.org.br/main.php?id_menu=4&cd_language=2).

RESOURCES

This is a small selection of websites for those seeking more information on the World Social Forum and social forum processes.

Social Forums

World Social Forum (http://www.worldsocialforum.org/), the WSF's main website with information and updates on forums around the world.

U.S. Social Forum (http://www.ussf2007.org/), website for the first national social forum in the United States.

Americas Social Forum (http://www.forosocialamericas.org/), with information (in Spanish) on the continental forums in Quito (2004) and Caracas (2006).

Midwest Social Forum (http://www.mwsocialforum.org/), an annual gathering of grassroots organizations, community activists, and others.

Boston Social Forum (http://www.bostonsocialforum.org/), 2004 meeting of social movements.

Border Social Forum (http://www.forosocialfronterizo.com/), transnational social forum held in Ciudad Juárez/El Paso in October
2006.

Documents

World Social Forum Charter of Principles (http://www.forum
socialmundial.org.br/main.php?id_menu=4&cd_language=2), a
document that organizations that comprised the World Social
Forum Organizing Committee drafted in 2001 that has largely
defined the WSF's ideological orientation. (See also the Appendix
in this volume.)

Porto Alegre Manifesto (http://www.zmag.org/sustainers/content/
2005-02/20group_of_nineteen.cfm), a proposal for social change
drafted by a group of nineteen notable figures at the 2005 World
Social Forum.

Bamako Appeal (http://www.openspaceforum.net/twiki/tikiindex
.php?page=Bamakoappeal), drafted in 2006 at the Polycentric
Forum in Mali, and aims to contribute to the gains made at that
forum.

Organizations and Groups

North American Research Workshop on the World Social Forum
Process (http://www.nd.edu/~wsfgroup/), collaborative website
for the group of scholar-activists who wrote this book.

DEMOS Project (http://demos.iue.it/), study of European-based
social movement activity, including that related to the social forum
process.

Network Institute for Global Democratization (http://www.nigd.org),
an international network working on radical democracy and one
of the instigators of the WSF.

ABOUT THE AUTHORS

Marc Becker teaches Latin American History at Truman State University. His research focuses on constructions of race, class, and gender within popular movements in the South American Andes. He has a forthcoming book on the history of indigenous movements in twentieth-century Ecuador. He is an Organizing Committee member of the Midwest Social Forum (MWSF), a Steering Committee member and web editor for Historians Against the War (HAW), and a member of the Network Institute for Global Democratization (NIGD).

Dorval Brunelle is professor of sociology and director of the Observatory of the Americas at the University of Quebec in Montreal (UQAM). He has published extensively on Quebec and the Canadian political economy, law and social exclusion, and social dimensions of globalization. His latest book, *Dérive globale*, has been translated into English as *From World Order to Global Disorder: States, Markets, and Dissent* (2007). Brunelle has edited or coedited numerous books on global integration, and his current research addresses the World Social Forum process and market liberalization and gender issues.

Christopher Chase-Dunn is Distinguished Professor of Sociology and director of the Institute for Research on World-Systems at the

University of California–Riverside. He is the author of *Rise and Demise: Comparing World-Systems* (with Thomas D. Hall), *The Wintu and Their Neighbors* (with Kelly Mann), and *The Spiral of Capitalism and Socialism* (with Terry Boswell). He is the founder and coeditor (with Walter Goldfrank) of the *Journal of World-Systems Research*. Chase-Dunn is currently doing research on global elite integration in the nineteenth century and on both the growth and decline phases and upward sweeps of empires and future global state formation.

Donatella della Porta is professor of sociology at the European University Institute. Among her recent publications are *Globalization from Below* (2006); *Quale Europa? Europeizzazione, identità e conflitti* (2006); *Social Movements: An Introduction*, 2nd edition (2006); and *Transnational Protest and Global Activism* (2005).

Rosalba Icaza Garza is a Marie Curie Post-Doctoral Research Fellow at the Iberoamerican Institute, Gothenburg University in Sweden. She acts as an external associate of the Centre for the Study of Globalization and Regionalization (CSGR). Her forthcoming *Globalizations* article is entitled "To Be and Not to Be: The Question of Transborder Civic Activism and Regionalization in Mexico. A Critical Account of Neo-Gramscian Perspectives."

Jeffrey S. Juris is assistant professor of anthropology in the Department of Social and Behavioral Sciences at Arizona State University. He received his PhD in anthropology from the University of California–Berkeley, where his research explored globalization, social movements, and transnational activism. His forthcoming book, *Networking Futures* (2008), explores the cultural logic and politics of transnational networking among anticorporate globalization activists in Barcelona. He has also published several articles regarding this topic as well as the relationship between new digital technologies and grassroots social movements.

Marina Karides is assistant professor of sociology at Florida Atlantic University. She is an active participant in the World Social Forums and Sociologists Without Borders. Her recent work considers gendered dimensions of globalization and the global justice movement. She has published articles in *Social Problems, Social Development Issues,* and *International Sociology and Social Policy* and multiple chapters that critically examine microenterprise development and the plight of informally self-employed persons in the global south. She is currently writing a book on street vendors and spatial rights in the global economy.

Lorenzo Mosca is Max Weber fellow at the European University Institute of Florence and collaborates in the DEMOS project (http://demos.eui.eu) with Donatella della Porta. Among his recent publications are "Contamination in Action and the Global Justice Movement" (with Donatella della Porta) in *Global Networks* (January 2007); *Globalization from Below: Transnational Activists and Protest Networks* (with Donatella della Porta, Massimiliano Andretta, and Herbert Reiter) (2006); and (with Massimiliano Andretta) "Understanding the Genoa Protest," in R. Taylor (ed.), *Interpreting Global Civil Society* (2004).

Ellen Reese is associate professor of sociology at the University of California–Riverside. Her research focuses on poverty, welfare state development, urban politics, and social movements. Her book *Backlash Against Welfare Mothers: Past and Present* (2005) examines long-term transformations in the U.S. welfare state. She is also coeditor with Amalia Cabezas and Marguerite Waller of *The Wages of Empire: Neoliberal Policies, Repression, and Women's Poverty* (Paradigm Publishers, 2007). She is currently writing a new book, *They Say Cutback; We Say Fightback! Welfare Rights Activism in an Era of Retrenchment.*

Jackie Smith is associate professor of sociology and peace studies at the University of Notre Dame. She is author of *Global Visions/Rival Networks: Social Movements for Global Democracy* (2008). She has coedited three books and numerous articles on transnational activism, including *Coalitions Across Borders: Transnational Protest in a Neoliberal Era* (with Joe Bandy), which explores how people have developed organizations and techniques to build transnational alliances among people of widely varying cultural, political, and economic backgrounds.

Peter (Jay) Smith is professor of political science at Athabasca University, Alberta, Canada. He has published recent articles on themes including new communications technologies, globalization and trade politics, transnational organizing, democracy, and citizenship. His work has appeared in *Global Governance: A Review of Multilateralism and International Organizations* and in numerous edited volumes, including *eTransformation in Governance: New Directions in Government and Politics* (edited by Mattie Malkia, Ari-Veikko Anttiroiko, and Reijo Savolainen) and *A Hundred Years of Citizenship in Australia and Canada* (edited by Pierre Boyer, Linda Cardinal, and David Heaton).

Rolando Vázquez is visiting fellow at the Sociology Department, University of Warwick in the UK and at the Sociology Department, Gothenburg University in Sweden. He has done research on the temporality of the political, by linking the works of Hannah Arendt and Walter Benjamin. In 2006 he published "Thinking the Event with Hannah Arendt," *European Journal of Social Theory* 9(1): 43–57. He is completing research on the temporality of globalization and on the relationship between art and the commodity.

INDEX

Titles in the Series

The Rules of the Game: A Primer on International Relations
by Mark R. Amstutz
A Tale of Two Quagmires: Iraq, Vietnam, and the Hard Lessons of War
by Kenneth J. Campbell
Celebrity Diplomacy
by Andrew F. Cooper
People Count! Individuals in Global Politics
by James N. Rosenau
Paradoxes of Power: U.S. Foreign Policy in a Changing World
edited by David Skidmore